John Brown

Height

N

W   E

S

B. & O. R. R.

River →

To Frederick
20 miles

Map of Harpers
Ferry

LUCY KROLL AGENCY
119 WEST 57th STREET
NEW YORK 19, N. Y.
PL 7-4250

PUBLICATION DATE: MAY 1st, 1970

JOHN BROWN:

The Sword and The Word

By
BARRIE STAVIS

Plays
Lamp at Midnight
The Man Who Never Died
Harpers Ferry
Coat of Many Colors
Refuge

Fiction
Home, Sweet Home!
The Chain of Command

John Brown

JOHN BROWN:

The Sword and The Word

by
BARRIE STAVIS

South Brunswick and New York: A. S. Barnes and Company
London: Thomas Yoseloff Ltd

A. S. Barnes and Co., Inc.
Cranbury, New Jersey 08512

Thomas Yoseloff Ltd
108 New Bond Street
London W1Y OQX, England

SBN 498 07520 6
Printed in the United States of America

For my noble son, Alex
and
My lovely daughter, Jane
and
For my wife, Bernice.

A NOTE FROM THE PUBLISHER

John Brown: The Sword and the Word is a companion volume to Barrie Stavis's play, *Harpers Ferry*. This powerful and profoundly engrossing play about John Brown had the distinction in 1967 of being the first new play presented by the Tyrone Guthrie Theatre, Minneapolis, Minnesota, and was directed by Tyrone Guthrie. While *John Brown: The Sword and the Word* and *Harpers Ferry* are independent works, they reinforce each other. The reader of this present volume will be interested to see how in *Harpers Ferry* the author has taken the raw documents of history, has penetrated and unified them, until finally a work of art emerges.

In addition to the general reader, theatre workers preparing a production of *Harpers Ferry*—director, actor, scenic artist and costume designer—will find *John Brown: The Sword and the Word* invaluable for background material necessary to mount a production.

CONTENTS

INTRODUCTORY REMARKS AND
ACKNOWLEDGMENTS

This book is intended for the general reader. While it is hoped that the historian and scholar of the period will find much of interest, it is the general reader whom I address. For this reason, I have not used footnotes; nor will the reader find a single *ibid., op. cit., loc. cit., et al., vide* or *idem* in the entire volume! Instead, I have incorporated the sources of the important material directly into the work itself. The reader who wishes to explore further will find a bibliography in the back of the book.

Too many people shy away from a formidable looking book they would otherwise read, and would *enjoy* reading, if it were not quite so forbidding and overfreighted with footnotes. The story of John Brown is too central to both the 19th and 20th Centuries, and the parallels between John Brown's time and ours too startling, to be so sequestered.

To achieve greater flow of the narrative, I have frequently cut the documents quoted but have not used the traditional three and four dots to indicate an ellipsis. In no instance have I altered the meaning.

In John Brown's day "Harpers" was spelled with an apostrophe "s". I have therefore used "Harper's" in original documents; in my own writing I have used the contemporary spelling, "Harpers."

* * * * * *

[9]

It is customary when acknowledging one's indebtedness to the various people who have helped bring a book to life, to list all the people and then conclude with a thanks to one's wife (or husband). I, too, have several times followed this custom. *This* time, my first acknowledgment is for my wife, Bernice. Her courage and integrity, her judgment and downright good sense which is combined with honor and wit remain for me a marvel of the human spirit. Her hand is fixed on every page of the book.

My profound thanks to Boyd B. Stutler and Dr. Herbert Aptheker. These two men, separated in life experience and temperament, are united by their vast knowledge of John Brown and their understanding of his importance in our history. My correspondence with Mr. Stutler, whose knowledge of John Brown is awesome, stretches out over many years; my letters querying him always received a prompt reply, giving me fact and figure in detail. After sending him the final draft, I received his most welcome letter of May 7, 1969, which begins with, "I have given your *John Brown: The Sword and the Word* a very careful reading and have found less to criticize, correct, suggest changes or make critical comment than in any other. The manuscript reflects broad research and careful handling of materials, which, as I know, covered many years. I recall one pleasant afternoon in October, 1959, when we sat on the porch of the Hill Top House at Harpers Ferry and discussed plans for this work . . . "

My many thanks to my cousin, Ben Stavis. He made himself continually available for discussion and advice during the writing of the book, and he worked the manuscript through twice, each time giving me of his own invaluable insights and experience. Elly Weiss and B. J. Whiting worked with me editorially. I shall never be able to repay their devotion and concern. Probing and tough, they forced me into sharper thinking, thus enabling me to bring the work into greater clarity and focus.

Many other people helped this book along the way: Dr.

Karl Menninger, Dr. Herbert Schlesinger, Sir Tyrone Guthrie, Dr. Clarence S. Gee, Morton Stavis, Esther Stavis, Rosann Stavis, Adelaide Bean, Raymond Bechtle, John Lewin, Hazel Lewin, Dr. Howard Selsam, Stephen Gray, Thea Gray, Joseph Reichbart, Angus Cameron, Howard N. Meyer, Mary Winters, Dr. Louis Ruchames, Julian Schlossberg and Arthur Levine, Ernest Kaiser of the Schomburg Collection of the New York Public Library gave of his time and counsel in the selection of the pictures. A special and warm greeting to my editor, Nina Shoehalter, who saw the book through its rough spots—and became my friend in the process. And, finally my gratitude and appreciation to Norman Weinstein, who went through the entire manuscript and gave me generously of his invaluable knowledge and experience.

Barrie Stavis

June 1, 1969
New York City

Was John Brown simply an episode, or was he an eternal truth? And if a truth, how speaks that truth today?
John Brown loved his neighbor as himself. He could not endure therefore to see his neighbor poor, unfortunate or oppressed. This natural sympathy was strengthened by a saturation in Hebrew religion which stressed the personal responsibility of every human soul to a just God. To this religion of equality and sympathy with misfortune, was added the strong influence of the social doctrines of the French Revolution with its emphasis on freedom and power in political life. And on all this was built John Brown's own inchoate but growing belief in a more just and a more equal distribution of property. From this he concluded,—and acted upon that conclusion— that all men are created free and equal, and the cost of liberty is less than the price of repression.

John Brown by W. E. B. DuBois

Part I

"But as I love my life, I would side with the light and let
the dark earth roll from under me, calling my mother and my
brother to follow."

Henry David Thoreau:
Slavery in Massachusetts.

John Brown was born on May 9, 1800, in Torrington,
Connecticut. He was hanged on December 2, 1859, in
Charlestown, Virginia, [now Charles Town, West Vir-
ginia] the first American since the nation was founded to
be hanged as a traitor.

Genealogists differ as to his ancestry. One group holds
that he stemmed from Peter Brown who arrived on the
Mayflower; another school holds that this particular Peter
Brown was not a forebear of the John Brown we are discussing. But no matter; certainly John Brown's forebears
on both sides landed in America sometime during the 17th
Century. His mother, Ruth Mills, came from 17th Century
Dutch settlers. Both of John Brown's grandfathers fought
in the Revolutionary War; his paternal grandfather, also
named John Brown, died in the Revolutionary War in the
year 1776.

John Brown's father, Owen, was firmly opposed to
slavery. He ran a station in the underground railroad; on
his premises he had a secret place for hiding runaway

slaves as they were passed from station to station northward to freedom—sometimes to the northern sections of
the United States, but frequently to Canada.

In 1805, Owen Brown, John Brown's father, moved the
family from Torrington, Connecticut, to Hudson, Ohio.
This was wild country indeed—Indians, dangerous animals, poisonous snakes. James Fenimore Cooper, writing
of the wilderness of the United States at the turn of the
19th Century, described how a squirrel could ascend a
tree on the East Coast of the United States and traverse
the full 3,000 miles to the West Coast, hopping from tree
to tree, descending to the ground only to cross rivers and
the Great Plains.

Such was the American wilderness in 1800, and Hudson,
Ohio, was a sparsely settled village in this wilderness.
There, John Brown grew up—a self-reliant, strong boy,
who by the age of ten was already performing the tasks
of a grown man. Owen Brown was a tanner, and the boy,
John, helped in the tannery. Owen was also a shoemaker,
and John helped make shoes. And, of course, Owen was a
farmer, so John worked on the farm. He hunted, trapped,
dressed his own leather, made whiplashes which sometimes he was able to sell. He mixed with the Indians and
learned some of their language. His schooling was mini-
mal, though at the age of ten he had access to a library
in a neighbor's home and did a fair amount of reading.

John Brown's mother died when he was eight years old.
Although his father remarried a fine and good woman, she
was never able to replace John Brown's first loss. Many
years later, when he was 57, John Brown wrote a short
autobiographical sketch of his boyhood for the 12-year-old
son of a friend and fellow abolitionist. This sketch can be
found in Richard J. Hinton's *John Brown and His Men.*
In it he says: "He never adopted her in feelings; but continued to pine after his own mother for years."

Writing further about himself—always in the third person, he says: "This operated very unfavorably upon him,

[15]

as he was both naturally fond of females; and withall extremely diffident."

When the War of 1812 broke out, Owen Brown sold cattle to the troops. John Brown, aged 12, was often charged with the task of driving a herd all by himself, through the Ohio wilderness to the quartermaster depot a hundred miles away. He saw much corruption and venality during the War of 1812, and he writes further about himself in his informal autobiography:

> During this war he had some chance to form his own boyish judgment of men. The effect of what he saw was to so far disgust him with Military affairs that he would neither train, or drill; but paid fines; and got along like a Quaker untill his age finally had cleared him of Military duty.

This man, who was to figure prominently from 1856 to 1859 in military and political battles fought in Kansas Territory to determine whether the Territory would enter the United States as a free or slave state—this man who, in October, 1859, with a small band of 21 men, was to cross the river from Maryland into Virginia and attack the town of Harpers Ferry, taking possession of the Federal Government Armory and Arsenal there—this man in his youth would neither train nor drill, preferring to pay fines. He was, in effect, a conscientious objector. Indeed, so great was his antipathy to weapons, that when he had his own tannery, he would not sell leather to any man who entered his shop carrying a rifle.

There is a further paragraph of interest in his short autobiography:

> During the war with England a circumstance occurred that in the end made him a most determined Abolitionist; and led him to declare, or Swear: Eternal War with slavery. He was staying for a short time with a very gentlemanly landlord who held a slave boy near his own age very active, intelligent, and good feeling; and to whom John was under con-

siderable obligation for numerous little acts of kindness. The Master made a great pet of John; brought him to table with his friends; called their attention to every little smart thing he said or did; and to the fact of his being more than a hundred miles from home with a company of cattle alone; while the negro boy (who was fully if not more than his equal) was badly clothed, poorly fed; and lodged in cold weather; and beaten before his eyes with Iron Shovels or any other thing that came first to hand. This brought John to reflect on the wretched, hopeless condition, of Fatherless and Motherless slave children: for such children have neither Fathers or Mothers to protect, and provide for them. He sometimes would raise the question: is God their Father?

Owen Brown was a Congregationalist. At the age of 16, John Brown requested and received acceptance into the Congregational Church in Hudson. And at this age he decided to enter the ministry. With a brother and a friend, he traveled East and enrolled in a school in Plainfield, Massachusetts. The three stayed there for a few months and then went to Morris Academy in Litchfield, Connecticut, to prepare for entrance into a college where John Brown, steadfast to his desire, planned to study for the ministry. However, an eye inflammation prevented him from studying and his hopes were shattered. He returned to Hudson, Ohio, and went to work again for his father in the tannery.

What a minister John Brown would have made! What a soul-reaching effect he would have had on his congregation!

John Brown worked for his father until the age of 20. He became foreman of the tannery—assuredly because of ability, not nepotism. Nor should the size of the tannery be exaggerated. Five, perhaps ten, people worked there. During this period, he taught himself mathematics and became an expert surveyor. At various times in his life he was able to earn his living as a surveyor.

At the age of 20, John Brown set up his own tannery. That same year, he married his first wife, Dianthe Lusk.

Six years later, with his wife and three children, he moved to Pennsylvania. He settled on a site along the road east of Meadville because the area was rich in the bark needed for the tanning process. Deer, bear, turkey, all abounded, and the long howl of the wolf could frequently be heard at night. This was the beginnings of a town which John Brown named Randolph [now New Richmond]. He succeeded in establishing a post office there,

He remained in Randolph for nine years—from 1826 to 1835. These were his years of achievement and of material success. He cleared 25 acres of land; he built a tannery, so successful that it employed as many as 15 men; he built a log house and a barn; and like his father's, his barn had a and was appointed its first postmaster.

concealed room under the hayrick to hide runaway slaves; he bred cattle successfully, bringing in blooded stock from Hudson, Ohio, in 1828, as well as prime sheep and hogs. He had a great reputation for the quality of his leather, which was thoroughly dried of moisture, for, as he said, he would not sell water for leather. He established a reading community by circulating books and magazines; he built a school; he was the major force in organizing a church. At that time, the most laudatory thing one could say of a man was that "he was as enterprising and as honest as John Brown."

In those days, it was often the custom for an unmarried workingman to board in the home of his employer. Thus, John Brown's household often contained five to ten workmen as well as his own ever-growing family. George B. Delamater, who lived nearby during this period, describes how this household was run:

In the winter, breakfast was usually had before daylight, immediately after which Bibles were distributed—Brown requiring each one to read a given number of verses, himself leading; then he would stand up to pray, grasping the back of the chair at the top, and inclining slightly forward. After this members of the family dispersed to their respective pursuits.

There were also prayers in the evening. John Brown "seemed to be an inspired paternal ruler controlling and providing for the circle of which he was the head."

Throughout these years of prosperity and success, John Brown continually asked his neighbors for contributions for the relief of fugitive slaves. He also asked that they furnish hiding places as these fugitives were moved North along the Underground Railroad. He considered it as much his duty to help a Negro make his escape, as it was to help catch a horse thief.

There are some revealing stories about the John Brown of this Hudson, Ohio and Randolph, Pennsylvania period. In light of his later career, his work in Kansas, and his raid on Harpers Ferry, they are of great interest.

James Forman, who was employed by John Brown, tells the story of how one of John Brown's workmen stole a choice calfskin. John Brown discovered the theft. His lecture on honesty reduced the man to tears. Then John Brown informed the man that if he left his employment, he would be prosecuted for theft; but if he stayed on and continued to work, John Brown would not prosecute. The man elected to continue working. For the next two months, on John Brown's orders, no one in the house or the tannery was allowed to speak to this man, not to ask or answer a question, not even to bid him good morning or good evening. Two months of absolute silence to atone for an attempted theft.

James Forman also recounts the following story. John

Brown's wife became ill. He mounted his horse and galloped off for the doctor. On the way, he came across two men tying up bags of apples which they had stolen from an orchard and were preparing to put on their horses. John Brown dismounted, forced the men to empty their sacks and confess the intended theft. Having settled the matter, he remounted and went off to fetch the doctor for his sick wife.

And again from Forman we hear how a man stole a cow and was apprehended. He pleaded poverty. The owner, having retrieved his cow and feeling sorry for the would-be thief, decided not to press charges. The next day John Brown heard of the incident, called in a constable and had the thief re-arrested. The man was committed to jail for several months. During the entire time that he was in prison, John Brown regularly supplied the prisoner's family with an abundance of provisions so that they would not want. He maintained that the man had committed a crime and must be punished, but the family was innocent and therefore should not suffer for the man's wrongdoing.

And finally from Forman, we hear the story of how, during a heavy winter when little work was to be had, John Brown heard a rumor that a family several miles away was destitute. Knowing that the man in question was proud, John Brown sent one of his workmen and wife to pay what was ostensibly a social call but in reality was to assess the situation. The workman reported that there was indeed poverty and hunger in the family. Knowing that the man wouldn't take charity, John Brown came to him with a business proposition. He offered the man provisions and clothing in exchange for his labor during the next summer. Came the summer, John Brown did not pick up his end of the arrangement—nor had he ever intended to. This was his way of tiding the family over a bad winter.

John Brown became a teetotaler at the age of 29; from

that year on, he never touched alcohol. The story of how he became an abstainer was told by one of his sons, Salmon Brown, many years later:

> While he was living in Pennsylvania it was the custom for every farmer to have a barrel of whiskey in the house. It was also the custom to have "bees" and barn-raisings. A tavern-keeper was to have a barn-raising, and father was to be there. The tavern-keeper needed more liquor and sent to Meadville by father, then scarcely in middle life, for a three-gallon jug. The liquor cost twenty-five cents a gallon. On the road from Meadville father became thirsty and began taking "nips" from the jug. He was accustomed to drinking from his own barrel, and did not think the practice wrong. On the way to the barn-raising father realized that liquor was getting hold of him, and he became alarmed. He reasoned that if liquor would lead him to drink from another man's jug it was surely gaining control over him—a thing he could not allow. Coming to a large rock by the roadway, he smashed the jug upon it, vowing that he would not be responsible for his neighbor's drinking at the barn-raising, where accidents might happen. He paid for the liquor, and when he reached home rolled his whiskey barrel into the backyard and smashed it to pieces with an ax. No liquor was allowed about the house afterwards.

When John Brown's eldest son, John Brown, Jr., was an adult, he wrote some recollections of his boyhood. One of these concerns a series of revival meetings which the family attended:

> There were a number of free colored persons and some fugitive slaves. These became interested and came to the meetings, but were given seats by themselves, where the stove had stood, near the door—not a good place for seeing ministers or singers. Father noticed this, and when the next meeting had fairly opened, he rose and called attention to the fact, that, in seating the colored portion of the audience, a discrimination had been made, and said that he did not believe God is "a respecter of persons." He then invited the

colored people to occupy his slip. The blacks accepted, and all of our family took their vacated seats. The blacks during the remainder of that protracted meeting continued to occupy our slip, and our family the seats around the stove.

The last of these stories is also taken from the reminiscences of John Brown, Jr. Here he describes a somewhat different incident:

My first apprenticeship to the tanning business consisted of grinding bark with a blind horse. This became slightly monotonous. While the other children were out at play in the sunshine, where the birds were singing, I used to be tempted to let the old horse have a long rest. I did not fully appreciate the importance of a good supply of ground bark. The old blind horse, unless ordered to stop, would, like Tennyson's Brook, "go on forever," and thus keep up the appearance of business; but the creaking of the hungry mill would betray my neglect, and then father, hearing this from below, would come up and stealthily pounce upon me while I was at a window looking upon outside attractions. He finally grew tired of these frequent admonitions for my laziness and concluded to adopt with me a sort of book-account, something like this:—

John, Jr.,

    For disobeying mother . . . . . . 8 lashes
    For unfaithfulness at work . . . . . 3 lashes
    For telling a lie . . . . 8 lashes

On a certain Sunday morning he invited me to accompany him from the house to the tannery, saying that he had concluded it was time for a settlement. After a long and tearful talk over my faults, he again showed me my account, which exhibited a fearful footing up of debits. I had no credits or off-sets, and was of course bankrupt. I then paid about one-third of the debt, reckoned in strokes from a nicely-prepared blue-beech switch, laid on "masterly". Then, to my utter astonishment, father stripped off his shirt, and, seating himself on a block, gave me the whip and bade me "lay it on" to his bare back. I dared not refuse to obey, but at first I did not strike hard. "Harder!" he said, "harder, harder!" until he

[22]

received the balance of the account. Small drops of blood showed on his back where the tip end of the tingling beech cut through. Thus ended the account and settlement, which was also my first practical illustration of the Doctrine of the Atonement. I was then too obtuse to perceive how Justice could be satisfied by inflicting penalty upon the back of the innocent instead of the guilty; but at that time I had not read the ponderous volumes of Jonathan Edwards' sermons which father owned.

Jonathan Edwards of the 18th Century, John Brown of the 19th Century, Martin Luther King, Jr., of the 20th Century—men preaching that the sin of the world can be lessened, perhaps atoned for, by the injured one taking on, even embracing, the punishment due the sinner. This, of course, is the doctrine enunciated in Isaiah 53:5. "He was bruised for our iniquities; upon Him was the chastisement that made us whole; and with His stripes we are healed."

The same pattern prevails in all these stories: intense social concern for other people, often at his own expense and that of his family; a high-handed, often arbitrary way of seeing justice done—as he understood justice; a pitting of his own acute sense of morality and ethics against the complacency of others.

In 1834, John Brown wrote to his brother, Frederick, who was still living in Hudson, Ohio. This letter, to be found in Franklin Benjamin Sanborn's *Life and Letters of John Brown,* is of particular interest because it was the first time he put into writing a plan to help slaves:

I have been trying to devise some means whereby I might do something in a practical way for my poor fellow-men who are in bondage, and having fully consulted the feelings of my wife and my three boys, we have agreed to get at least one negro boy or youth, and bring him up as we do our own,—viz., give him a good English education, learn him what we can about the history of the world, about business, about general subjects, and, above all, try to teach him the fear of God. We think of three ways to obtain one: First, to try to get some Christian slaveholder to release one to us. Second, to get a free one if no one will let us have one that is a slave. Third, if that does not succeed, we have all agreed to submit to considerable privation in order to buy one.

This has been with me a favorite theme of reflection for years. Perhaps we might, under God, in that way do more towards breaking their yoke effectually than in any other. If the young blacks of our country could once become enlightened, it would most assuredly operate on slavery like firing powder confined in rock, and all slaveholders know it well. Witness their heaven-daring laws against teaching blacks. If once the Christians in the free States would set to work in earnest in teaching the blacks, the people of the slave-holding States would find themselves constitutionally driven to set about the work of emancipation immediately.

Here we see the shape of John Brown's thinking. He recognized that enforced ignorance was a weapon used very consciously by the slaveowner; it was a penal offense to teach a slave to read. He saw education as the lever which could force the slaveowner to extend freedom to the slaves. He would therefore get a black youth and raise him in his house as one of his own children. The key was to be education and a model school which would encourage others in the North to found similar schools.

This letter was written when the issue of slavery, although sharply debated, did not yet dominate the national scene. Exactly 25 years later, in 1859, John Brown made his famous raid on Harpers Ferry. In the intervening years the Fugitive Slave Law had been passed, battles had been fought to bring Kansas Territory into the Union as a free state, the Dred Scott Decision had been handed down by the Supreme Court; the issue had sharpened so that many on both sides knew they were drawing closer to the impending conflict. By 1859, in fact, long before that, John Brown was convinced that the slaveholder would fight to the death to maintain the institution of slavery because the whole fabric of his society rested on his ownership of property in the shape of human beings. In the 1850s, there were four million slaves in the United States having an average worth of a thousand dollars each; thus, the slave system had an investment of four billion dollars in human property. This investment generated a profit of between 500 million and 750 million dollars a year. (When Lincoln signed the Emancipation Proclamation on January 1, 1863, he prepared the way to strip the South of four billion dollars in capital, and of one-half to three-quarters of a billion dollars in annual income. The passage of the Thirteenth Amendment effectively accomplished this purpose.) Long before 1859, John Brown had come to realize that education for the slave was not the key; the only way to destroy the system was by the *sword*.

*   *   *   *   *   *

John Brown's years of success and family life, from 1825 to 1834, were not unalloyed. In the spring of 1831, a boy, aged four, died. In 1832, John Brown's wife, Dianthe, gave birth to a son, the seventh child in their 12 years of marriage. The child died a few hours after birth. Dianthe died the next day. John Brown writes to his father, with whom he always had a warm and tender relationship:

We are again smarting under the rod of our Heavenly Father. Last night about eleven o'clock my affectionate, dutiful and faithful Dianthe bade "farewell to Earth".

The letter ends: "Tomorrow she is to lay beside our little son. From your sorrowing son, John Brown."

Mary was John Brown's second wife. They met in 1832, the year his first wife died. John Brown, 32 years old, had been left with the sole care of his five remaining children. To help out in the household, he took in Mary Anne Day, daughter of a blacksmith. She was 16, tall and strong. John Brown became attracted to her.

In John Brown's short autobiography written in the third person, he described himself as "naturally fond of females; and withall diffident." His proposal of marriage to Mary Anne Day is a perfect example of this combination of affection and diffidence. He proposed to her in a letter. The next day he followed her to the spring when she went to get water for the household, and there at the spring asked for her answer. They were married 11 months to the day of Dianthe's death, and this 17-year-old wife became stepmother to five children, the eldest of whom was only four years younger than she.

Only a woman of the greatest strength and courage could have stood side by side with John Brown for the next 26 years until he was hanged in 1859 for the raid on Harpers Ferry. A year after their marriage, Mary Brown gave birth to her first child; 20 years later, in 1854, she gave birth to her thirteenth. John Brown was 54 years old when his last child was born; Mary was 38.

John Brown was to "smart under the rod of his Heavenly Father" many more times. In 1843, *four* children from his second marriage died in a period of 12 days, all stricken down by an epidemic of dysentery. The ages of these children were nine, six, three and one.

He writes to his oldest son, John Brown, Jr.:

God has seen fit to visit us with the pestilence since you left us, and four of our number sleep in the dust. On the 4th, Charles was taken with dysentery and died on the 11th, about the time that Charles died Sarah, Peter, and Austin were taken with the same complaint. Austin died on the 21st, Peter on the 22nd, and Sarah on the 23rd, and were all buried together in one grave. They all now lie in a little row together. This has been to us all a bitter cup indeed, and we have drunk deeply.

Owen Brown, Sr., father of John Brown.

John Brown's birthplace in Torrington, Connecticut.

Early portrait of John Brown.

Portrait (1858).

Mary Ann Brown, wife of John Brown. Their daughters, Annie (left) and Sarah (right). Probably taken in 1851. (From the collection of Boyd B. Stutler.)

Three years later, in 1846, Amelia, who was born the year before, was accidentally scalded to death. John Brown, who was away from home on business, writes:

My Dear afflicted wife and children: one more dear little feeble child I am to meet no more till the dear, small and great shall stand before God.

And he ends his letter with: "A brighter day shall dawn; and let us not sorrow as those that have no hope."

His eldest daughter, Ruth, at that time 17, had been responsible for the accidental scalding of the infant, Amelia, and in this letter he cautions his family:

I trust that none of you will feel disposed to cast an unreasonable blame on my dear Ruth on account of the dreadful trial we are called upon to suffer.

As Ruth grew up he watched her with a tender mixture of concern and pride. One year after this dreadful accident, John Brown, again away from home, writes to Ruth:

I will just tell you what questions exercise my mind in regard to an absent daughter, and I will arrange them somewhat in order as I feel most their importance.

What feelings and motives govern her? In what manner does she spend her time? Who are her associates? How does she conduct in word and action? Is she improving generally? Is she provided for with such things as she needs, or is she in want? Does she enjoy herself, or is she lonely and sad? Is she among real friends, or is she disliked and despised? Such are some of the questions which arise in the mind of a certain anxious father; and if you have a satisfactory answer to them in your own mind, he can rest satisfied.

John Brown continued to "smart under the rod of his Heavenly Father." Two and one half years later, in 1849, an infant girl of 11 months died. Ruth describes the death:

In the fall of 1848, the little babe took a violent cold that ended in quick consumption, and she died at the end of April, 1849. Father spared no pains in doing all that medical skill could do for her, together with the tenderest care and nursing. The time that he could be at home was mostly spent in caring for her. He sat up nights to keep an even temperature in the room, and to relieve mother from the constant care which she had through the day. He used to walk with the child and sing to her so much that she soon learned his step. When she heard him coming up the steps to the door, she would reach out her hands and cry for him to take her. He noticed a change in her one morning, and told us he thought she would not live through the day, and came home several times to see her. A little before noon he came home, and looked at her and said, "She is almost gone." She heard him speak, opened her eyes, and put up her little wasted hands with such a pleading look for him to take her that he lifted her from the cradle, with the pillows she was lying on, and carried her until she died. He was very calm, closed her eyes, folded her hands, and laid her in her cradle. When she was buried, father broke down completely, and sobbed like a child. It was very affecting to see him so overcome, when all the time before his great tender heart had tried to comfort our weary, sorrowing mother, and all of us.

Three years after that, an infant boy, less than a month old, died. All told, nine children were lost in infancy and early childhood. In addition to these, he was to lose three sons in his fight against slavery. Frederick was killed in Kansas in 1856 at the age of 26; two other sons, Watson, 24, and Oliver, 20, were both killed in the raid on Harpers Ferry.

John Brown had seven children by his first wife and thirteen by his second; of these twenty children, but eight survived; four from the first marriage and four from the second. Little wonder that in 1852 John Brown writes to his daughter, Ruth:

[28]

My attachments to this world have been very strong, and Divine Providence has been cutting me loose, one cord after another. Up to the present time, notwithstanding that I have so much to remind me that all this must soon be severed, I am still clinging like those who have hardly taken a single lesson.

Little wonder then, that in prison in Charlestown, Virginia, sentenced to be hanged, John Brown writes to his wife, Mary: "Try to build up the broken walls of our once great family and make the utmost of every stone that is left."

But then, he cautions: "But, beloved ones, do remember that this is not your rest,—that in this world you have no abiding place or continuing city."

As for Mary Brown, when she learned of the failure of the raid on Harpers Ferry, and the wounding and capture of her husband, plus the death of her two sons, Oliver and Watson, she said:

Does it seem as if freedom were to gain or lose by this? I have had thirteen children, and only four are left; but if I am to see the ruin of my house, I cannot but hope that Providence may bring out of it some benefit to the poor slaves.

＊　＊　＊　＊　＊　＊

In 1835, John Brown moved to Franklin Mills, Ohio, now Kent, to set up a partnership in a tannery with Zenas Kent, a wealthy man of that area. The arrangements for the partnership foundered and John Brown began to involve himself in land purchases—actually, land speculation. Had he been able to hold out, he would have emerged a wealthy man, for land around Kent later became quite valuable. However, the depression of 1837 bankrupted him and from that year on, he was never out of debt.

[29]

Why should a man like John Brown speculate in land? He was a man of principle. How then, did he let himself get trapped into such excess? In part, he succumbed to the fever of the times; a swelling population rapidly pushing westward, trying to become rich overnight. In good part, however, John Brown wanted money for his fight against slavery. There were many instances when the family saved for some household necessity, but when the money was finally accumulated, John Brown would call a family conference and inform them that he had the money. What would they have him do: buy the object or use the money for the fight against slavery? The answer was always the same: use the money for the cause. Thus, they lived modestly, ate simply, though plentifully—were always saving, but never had money.

During the next five years, from 1837 to 1842, John Brown tried his hand at everything to provide for his continually increasing family; tanning, raising sheep, breeding race horses, buying cattle and driving them for sale to the markets in the East. He made two trips to the East with cattle, one in 1838 and the other in 1839. These were the first times he was away from his family for any lengthy period and they mark the beginning of many such trips. At first they were involved with business and his attempts to get out of debt and provide for his family. Later, they were concerned entirely with the destruction of slavery. During the first two trips he wrote a number of letters home. In them we find, as in so many of his later letters, his lonesomeness for his family and his desire to be with them. He writes:

My unceasing and anxious care for the present and ever-lasting welfare of every member of my family seems to be three-fold as I get separated farther and farther from them.

This lonesomeness continued without abatement; indeed, it seemed to increase as time and circumstance separated him more and more often from his family. On November 28, 1850, he writes from Springfield, Massachusetts:

At here and almost all places where I stop, I am treated with all kindness and attention; but it all does not make home. I feel lonely and restless no matter how neat and comfortable my room and bed, nor how richly loaded may be the table; they have very few charms for me, away from home. I can look back to our log Cabin at the Centre of Richfield with a supper of Porridge, and Johnny Cakes, as to a place of far more interest to me than the Massasoit of Springfield.

We also find in his letters a deep concern to reach closer to his wife and children, especially his children. He writes: "Forgive the many faults and foibles you have seen in me, and try to profit by anything good in either my example, or my counsel."

John Brown struggled unsuccessfully for five years to get himself out of debt. In 1842 he was declared bankrupt. For years afterwards he was hounded by all sorts of law suits. His affairs were terribly jumbled, and it is difficult to follow the skein of these complications. Bear in mind that in 1843, one year after his bankruptcy, he lost four of his children within a space of two weeks. He was indeed sorely beset by both personal and financial misfortunes during this period.

In 1847, writing from Springfield, Massachusetts, where he was involved in a wool business—a business which was to fail a few years later, leaving behind a trail of further debts and law suits both for himself, his partner and the firm, he begins a letter to Mary as follows:

It is once more Sabbath evening and nothing so much accords with my feelings as to spend a portion of it conversing with the partner of my own choice, and the sharer of my poverty, trials, discredit, and sore afflictions for quite a number of years. I do not forget the firm attachment of her who has remained my fast, and faithful affectionate friend. When I reflect on these things together with the verry considerable difference in our age, as well as all the follies, and faults with which I am justly chargeable, I really admire your constancy. If the large boys do wrong call them alone into your room, and expostulate with them kindly, and see if you cannot reach them by a kind but powerful appeal to their honor. I do not claim that such a theory accords verry much with my practice. I frankly confess it does not; but I want your face to shine even if my own should be dark, and cloudy. I feel considerable regret that I have lived so many years, and in reality have done so verry little to increase the amount of human happiness. It is my growing resolution to endeavor to promote my own happiness by doing what I can to render those around me more so.

John Brown's cast of mind begins to alter more strongly during this period. Surely it was conditioned by the fact that his business ventures turned into dust, one after another; but it was mainly determined by the growing pitch and passion on the question of slavery, which increased year by year with appalling ferocity.

The reason why slavery became a central issue may be found in the demographic shift of that period. In 1790, the population of the North and South were nearly even. By 1850, the year that the Fugitive Slave Law was passed, the population of the North was roughly 13.5 million, while that of the South was approximately 9.5 million. Smaller population notwithstanding, the South controlled the executive and judicial branches of the government. From 1789 to 1860, Southerners occupied the offices of the President, the Secretary of State, the Attorney General, and other cabinet posts for two-thirds of the time. In particular, the South controlled the offices of Secretary of War and Navy. Five of the nine justices of the Supreme Court, including the Chief Justice, were Southerners. The laws which emanated from Washington were designed not only to protect the institution of slavery, but to advance it.

[32]

It is a truism that wealth rules by reason of its inherent power, that the political state is partisan to men of property, that men of property will attempt to control a government in order to protect their interests. The political state eventually conforms to the facts of economic reality. When a new economic force rises and is not given proper political representation, it will achieve that recognition either by peaceful pressure or by the use of arms. As immigrants poured in and as wealth was created by the North, the South well understood its position. It knew what the census of 1870 would show, and could not afford to wait. This was part of the slaveholders' thinking when they determined to secede.

In 1850, the Fugitive Slave Law was passed, some in the North fighting the bill every step of the way. George Julian, a Northern member of the House of Representatives, said:

The passage of the Fugitive Slave Act will open a fresh wound in the North, and it will continue to bleed as long as the law stands unrepealed.

Henrietta Buckmaster, in her superb book on the Underground Railroad and the Abolition Movement, *Let My People Go*, details the provisions of the Fugitive Slave Law:

The identification of a fugitive could be made on the affidavit of a slave catcher without effort to substantiate his word. The fugitive could offer no defense, could not testify for himself. He was not allowed a trial by jury. The fee of the commissioner who settled the case was to be ten dollars if he found for the master and only five dollars if he freed the fugitive. If a Federal agent hampered in any way the seizure of a fugitive he was to be fined a thousand dollars, and if a fugitive escaped, with or without his help, he would be held responsible for the entire value of the slave. Bystanders could be forced to lend a hand if a fugitive tried to escape. And friends, in the underground work, or casual humanitarians, were liable to a fine of a thousand dollars or imprisonment for six months, if they were convicted of passing him on.

Many at that time felt that the slaveholding power in the South deliberately forced this brutal law through Congress as a tactical provocation. If the North refused to obey the law, the slaveocracy would have one more reason to secede.

Soon after the passage of the law, John Brown writes to his wife:

> It now seems that the Fugitive Slave Law was to be the means of making more Abolitionists than all the lectures we have had for years.

And he was right. In the North, people in all walks of life were outraged and repelled by a law which could force them to help a slave catcher—doubly so, when the slave catcher, merely by making out an affidavit could apprehend any Negro he wished, whether a fugitive slave or a free man. There were slave catchers who made a thriving business of scouting Northern towns for free Negroes with identifying marks. These slave catchers would return to the South where a fellow-conspirator used the description supplied by the slave catcher to swear out an affidavit that such and such a slave had escaped. The slave catcher, armed with the affidavit, would go back North, swear out a warrant and hire a few bullies to help him apprehend the Negro—really to abduct him. No black in the North, escaped or free, felt safe, for he never knew when he would be pounced upon and abducted into a life of slavery.

John Brown's response to the Fugitive Slave Law was one of direct action; he formed the League of Gileadites. This was an organization of Negroes and white friends designed to resist the Fugitive Slave Law. The program for the League was written out by John Brown, and can be found in Richard J. Hinton's *John Brown and His Men*. It begins with, "Nothing so charms the American people as personal bravery," and urging total resistance to slave catching, says:

> No jury can be found in the Northern States that would convict a man for defending his rights to the last extremity. This is well understood by Southern Congressmen, who insisted that the right of trial by jury should not be granted to the fugitive.

John Brown then gets down to specific tactics:

> Should one of your number be arrested, you must collect together as quickly as possible, so as to outnumber your adversaries. Let no able-bodied man appear on the ground unequipped, or with his weapons exposed to view.
> Do not delay one moment after you are ready. Let the first blow be the signal for all to engage. By going about your business quietly, you will get the job disposed of before the number that an uproar would bring together can collect; and you will have the advantage of those who come out against you, for they will be wholly unprepared with either equipments or matured plans; all with them will be confusion and terror.

Here he is expounding the principal doctrine of the commando raid. Choose the moment of attack and strike unexpectedly. Work rapidly, accomplish your task, and disappear before the enemy can bring up reinforcements. Though the total enemy force outnumbers you, *you* outnumber the enemy at the moment of strike—for you have a concentration of your forces, and the point you have selected for the attack is thinly held.

If things went wrong and the matter was brought to court, John Brown, in his recommendations to the League of Gileadites, has some interesting advice:

You may make a tumult in the court-room where a trial is going on, by burning gun-powder freely in paper packages if you cannot think of any better way to create a momentary alarm. But in such case the prisoner will need to take the hint at once, and bestir himself; and so should his friends improve the opportunity for a general rush.

And he has a final word of advice: "A lasso might possibly be applied to a slave catcher for once with good effect."

String up a couple of slave catchers for the effect it will have in deterring others from this nefarious trade. Here John Brown is advocating killing to achieve an ethical purpose.

John Brown, and all those who resisted the Fugitive Slave Law, were, of course, breaking the law of the land. They were thoroughly aware that they were breaking the law. In this they were following the position of Henry Thoreau, who, in turn, was in the direct tradition of William Godwin. In 1793, William Godwin had written his *Enquiry Concerning Political Justice And Its Influence On Morals and Happiness*, wherein he contended that too often moral law is disregarded in favor of political expediency, with a resultant economic advantage to a select few. Since moral law is fundamental and superior to the laws of government, every citizen not only may, but must set aside the law of the state if need be. It is his *duty* to follow the higher law of morality.

This rejection of unjust man-made law, this demand that every citizen declare and render allegiance to the higher law of morality, is precisely what Henry Thoreau advocated in his *Civil Disobedience,* published in 1849. Thoreau went to jail rather than have any part of the war against Mexico which would add slave territory to the United States. Said Thoreau in his *Civil Disobedience:*

It is not desirable to cultivate a respect for the law, so much as for the right. How does it become a man to behave toward this American government today? I answer, that he cannot without disgrace be associated with it. I cannot for an instant recognize that political organization as *my* government which is the *slave's* government also. [If the law] is of such a nature that it requires you to be an agent of injustice to another, then, I say, break the law. Let your life be a counter-friction to stop the machine.

Thousands of citizens of conscience disobeyed the Fugitive Slave Law as a matter of principle. Civil disobedience in the matter of principle and conscience is an American tradition which has survived countless jailings, beatings, hangings. During the early 1900s in the West, the Industrial Workers of the World, the I.W.W., resorted to mass civil disobedience in their Free Speech Fights in order to protect the rights of free speech.

Mahatma Gandhi acknowledged his indebtedness to Thoreau when Gandhi was evolving his strategy to achieve independence for India—passive mass resistance by so large a segment of the population that the machinery of the courts must break down under its impact. Present day struggle, where the strategy is nonviolent mass resistance, is in this same tradition.

Thoreau who, in 1849, advocated *passive* resistance to a government which he considered morally corrupt, only ten years later, in 1859, shifted his position so drastically that he embraced the action of John Brown and the raid on Harpers Ferry. He considered John Brown *the* great man of the century, a man who perfectly synthesized ethic with action. Thoreau's diary is replete with the anguish he felt as John Brown lay in prison. He was the first American to make a public statement in defense of John Brown. He knocked at doors, spoke to neighbors on the streets, invited them to come to Concord Town Hall to hear what he had to say.

In his address delivered before the citizens of Concord on October 30, 1859, during the very days that John Brown's trial was taking place in Charlestown, Virginia, Thoreau said:

[37]

He did not value his life in comparison with ideal things. He did not recognize unjust human laws, but resisted them as he was bid. For once we are lifted out of the trivialness and dust of politics into the region of truth and manhood. No man in America has ever stood up so persistently and effectively for the dignity of human nature, knowing himself for a man, and the equal of any and all governments. In that sense he was the most American of us all.

When I think of him and his six sons, and his son-in-law, not to enumerate the others, enlisted for this fight, proceeding coolly, reverently, humanely to work, for months if not years, sleeping and waking upon it, summering and wintering the thought, without expecting any reward but a good conscience, while almost all America stood ranked on the other side,—I say again it affects me as a sublime spectacle.

It was his peculiar doctrine that a man has a perfect right to interfere by force with the slaveholder, in order to rescue the slave. I agree with him. I shall not be forward to think him mistaken in his method who quickest succeeds to liberate the slave. I think that for once the Sharps rifles and the revolvers were employed in a righteous cause. The tools were in the hands of one who could use them.

This belief, "that a man has a perfect right to interfere by force with the slaveholder, in order to rescue the slave," was shared by The Reverend Theodore Parker, famous Unitarian minister and orator. Parker's position stemmed, as did John Brown's, from the conviction that slavery was a state of war in which a powerful majority exercised violence against a defenseless minority. Further, this institutionalized violence was sanctioned by the state. Slaves, therefore, were prisoners of war; in such a war, the minority has a right to avail itself of any and all means to achieve its rightful freedom. Parker forcefully expressed this concept in a letter to Francis Jackson, lawyer and powerful abolitionist. The letter was written from Rome, dated November 24, 1859, eight days before the scheduled hanging of John Brown; Jackson received it after the hanging. In it Parker said:

> It may be a natural duty for the freemen to help the slaves to the enjoyment of their liberty, and as a means to that end, to aid them in killing all such as oppose their natural freedom.

> If you were attacked by a wolf, I should not only have a right to aid you in getting rid of the enemy, but it would be my duty to help you in proportion to my power. If it were a murderer, and not a wolf who attacked you, the duty would be still the same. Suppose it is not a murderer who would kill you, but a kidnapper who would enslave, does that make it less my duty to help you out of the hands of your enemy? Suppose it is not a kidnapper who would make you a bondman, but a slaveholder who would keep you one, does that remove my obligation to help you?

Parker clearly foresaw the Civil War. In the same letter, he told Jackson:

> The American people will have to march to rather severe music, I think, and it is better for them to face it in season. A few years ago it did not seem difficult first to check slavery, and then to end it without any bloodshed. I think this cannot be done now, nor ever in the future. All the great charters of HUMANITY have been writ in blood. I once hoped that of American Democracy would be engrossed in less costly ink; but it is plain, now, that our pilgrimage must lead through a Red Sea, wherein many a Pharaoh will go under and perish. Alas! that we are not wise enough to be just, or just enough to be wise, and so gain much at small cost!

Part II

"I act from a principle. My aim and object is to restore human rights."

John Brown

In 1850, John Brown's business failed, utterly and completely. It took him four years to wind up his complicated affairs. He was in debt and remained in debt for the rest of his life. His economic state at the age of 50 was indeed in sharp contrast to the "paternal ruler" of the very large household he had maintained at the age of 30. Further, despite the many deaths which "the rod of his Heavenly Father" had seen fit to visit on him, he still had a large family to support. If ever a man could be called a failure, it would be he, John Brown—this 50-year-old man, graying rapidly, with a slight stoop to his shoulders. The appellation "Old Man" came naturally when people talked about him.

We come now to John Brown and Kansas. But in order to understand Kansas Territory of 1854, we must go back to 1820. In 1820, the Missouri Compromise was effected, prohibiting slavery north of 36 degrees, 30 minutes, North Latitude. However, the Kansas and Nebraska Act of May 30, 1854, allowed the settlers to decide for themselves whether slavery should or should not exist within the Territories. This act of 1854 was an abrogation of the 1820 Missouri Compromise which had *prohibited* slavery north of 36-30.

The North was especially incensed because only a few years earlier, in 1848, the peace treaty with Mexico had given the South all of Texas as well as other territory, and now the South was trying to make slave territory of Kansas, an area which had been expressly ruled out by the Missouri Compromise. The South, for its part, felt jeopardized if Kansas and Nebraska were ultimately to become free states. Illinois was to the east of Missouri and Iowa to its north, both free states; if Kansas and Nebraska, both to the west of Missouri, were to go free, then Missouri would be surrounded on three sides by free states, a dangerous situation.

Kansas Territory was opened on July 1, 1854, and settlers began to move in. At first, the South had everything its own way. It was simple for Missourians to cross the contiguous border and move into Kansas. It was also simple for settlers from Arkansas and Indian Territory [now Oklahoma] to move in. Not so with Easterners from New England, New York, Pennsylvania. It was a long and rough journey, and the final stretch, crossing through Missouri to get into Kansas, was the most difficult part of all. However, Emigrant Aid Societies began springing up in the North, raising money to send Free State men to Kansas to settle there and thus help to swing the impending vote against the South.

Three sons of John Brown, Owen, Frederick and Salmon, left for Kansas Territory with their families in October, 1854, and arrived during the spring of 1855. They had eleven head of cattle and three horses among them—their total wealth. On May 7, 1855, two more sons, Jason and John Brown, Jr., entered Kansas with a box of fruit trees, grape vines, a plow and other agricultural implements. They were home-seekers. True, they were interested in the cause of anti-slavery, but they were equally interested in the rich lands of Kansas Territory now open to them. During May of that year, a few weeks after he arrived, John Brown, Jr., wrote to his father:

> I know of no country where a poor man endowed with a share of common sense and with health, can get a start so easy. If we can succeed in making this a free State, a great work will be accomplished for mankind.

They came to settle, not to fight. They did not come into Kansas with arms. They had, among the five brothers, two small squirrel rifles and one revolver.

However, in this same letter, John Brown, Jr., wrote:

> I tell you the truth, when I say that while the interest of despotism has secured to its cause hundreds and thousands of the meanest and most desperate of men, armed to the teeth with Revolvers, Bowie Knives, Rifles and Cannon, the friends of freedom are not one fourth of them half armed.
>
> Miscreants which Missouri has ready at a moment's call to pour in upon them, boast they can obtain possession of the polls without having to fire a gun. Now Missouri is not alone in the undertaking to make this a Slave State. Every Slave-holding State from Virginia to Texas is furnishing men and money to fasten Slavery upon this glorious land, by means no matter how foul.
>
> Now the remedy we propose is, that the Anti-slavery portion of the inhabitants should immediately, thoroughly arm and organize themselves in military companies. In order to effect this, some persons must begin and lead in the matter.

John Brown, Jr., accurately described the situation. So intent were the pro-slavers upon driving the Free Staters out of Kansas Territory, that hundreds of well-armed Missourians made frequent raids across the border; they set fire to homes and crops, tarred and feathered, terrorized at the ballot box, and did not stop at murder. John Brown, Jr., felt that if the New Englanders were to be able to

[42]

establish a foothold in the Territory, they must organize and defend themselves. His letter goes on to itemize the weapons needed for such defense, and continues, "Now we want you to get for us these arms. We need them more than we do bread."

Less than a year before that, in August of 1854, when John Brown, Jr., wrote to his father that he and some of his brothers were planning to go to Kansas to settle, John Brown wrote back:

> If you or any of my family are disposed to go to Kansas or Nebraska, with a view to help defeat Satan and his legions in that direction, I have not a word to say; but I feel committed to operate in another part of the field. If I were not so committed, I would be on my way this fall.

We have no way of knowing to what other "part of the field" John Brown had committed himself. However, John Brown, Jr.'s detailed analysis of the situation in Kansas and the appeal for arms, moved the old man into action. He began speaking and collecting money with which to purchase arms for Kansas. Of equal importance, he himself began making preparations to journey into Kansas Territory.

The first election for a delegate to Congress from the Territory was held on November 29, 1854. Bonafide settlers from Missouri were there to vote. However, to their aid came swarms of residents of Missouri who cast 1,729 fraudulent ballots. As David R. Atchison, one of the Southern leaders, said:

> When you reside one day's journey of the Territory, and when your peace, your quiet and your property depend upon your action, you can without an exertion send five hundred of your young men who will vote in favor of your institutions. Should each county in the State of Missouri only do its duty, the question will be decided quietly and peaceably at the ballot-box.

Not only young men, but leading citizens of Missouri—lawyers, doctors, judges, merchants—were among the ballot-box stuffers. When the polls closed, they drove back to Missouri. The Howard Committee, authorized by Congress in March, 1856, to investigate the Kansas elections, found, for example, that in the Seventh District, 75 *miles* from the Missouri border, 604 votes were cast and 584 of these were illegal. Three months later, in February, 1855, the official census showed that a total of only 53 possible voters actually resided in that district. Missouri's position was summed up very well by a St. Louis paper:

This State would be flanked on the west with an unprincipled set of fanatics and negro-thieves, imported expressly to create annoyance, and disturb the social relations of the people of the frontier counties.

The Pawnee Legislature, elected by ballot-box stuffing, met in July, 1855, expelled the Free State members, and then adjourned to meet at Shawnee, two weeks later. This body, to be known henceforth as the Shawnee Legislature, promptly passed a series of laws against Free State men which betokened both hatred and fear:

(1) No one who opposed slavery could serve as a juror.
(2) Only pro-slavery men could hold office.
(3) The possession or distribution of literature which could disaffect a slave was punishable by five years at hard labor.
(4) The penalty for raising a rebellion among slaves was death.
(5) Voicing the belief that slavery was illegal in Kansas was punishable by five years or more at hard labor.

The Free Staters repudiated the bogus legislature, stating that it owed its existence to a combination of fraud and force. In answer to the Shawnee Legislature, the Free Staters held their own convention, of which John Brown,

[44]

Jr., was elected a vice-president. Further, as John Brown, Jr., wrote to his mother, he broke the law of the Shawnee Legislature by declaring in public:

> No man has a right to hold a slave in Kansas and further that if any officer should attempt to arrest me for a violation of this law and should put his villainous hands upon me, I would surely kill him so help me God.

The Shawnee Legislature and the Free State Convention were the beginning of dual government, charge and counter-charge, which plagued Kansas for several years. To add to the confusion and tangled skein of "Bleeding Kansas," the Free Staters were widely divided among themselves. In fact, there were two separate Free State Conventions, both held on the same day in Lawrence during August, 1855. One group was abolitionist, anxious to destroy slavery, root and stock. The other group was ready to make provision for the slaves already in the Territory and went on record that while Kansas should be a free white state, they favored "stringent laws excluding all Negroes, bond and free, from the Territory." One of the leaders of this second of the two Free State Conventions said: "So far as the rights of property are concerned, I know of no difference between the negro and the mule."

It was this situation—barely outlined here—that John Brown faced upon entering Kansas Territory on October 6, 1855, with a wagonload of arms and several followers, including his son, Oliver, the sixth of his sons who journeyed into Kansas, and his son-in-law, Henry Thompson. While waiting for the ferry to cross the Missouri River into Kansas, John Brown was told by a pro-slavery Missourian that he would never get to Kansas alive. He replied in his dry manner, "We are prepared not to die alone."

John Brown did not go into Kansas as a settler. He expected to remain possibly two or three years, right on the border fighting slavery, and then to move on to other areas. In point of fact, he remained 11 months and subsequently made two more trips to Kansas Territory.

When his party arrived in Kansas they had but sixty cents among them—but they had weapons. John Brown found the various members of his family in desperate condition. For food they had a little corn, some dried fruit, and a scant supply of potatoes. Their only shelter was tents. Winter was coming on, and worst of all, most of the men were sick with chills and fever.

For the first six weeks or so after his arrival in October, 1855, things were fairly quiet. John Brown and his sons built rude shanties to tide them over the winter, a winter so bitter that the temperature sometimes went down to 28 degrees below zero. These shanties consisted of three walls, made of tightly-bound-together prairie grass, pressed close to upright stakes. The fourth side was completely open. The roofs consisted of long shingles, loosely held together. Jason Brown and his family were more fortunate. Their home had four walls made of logs, and the roof consisted of a cotton sheeting. As Jason's wife wrote back to her mother-in-law, Mary Brown, in North Elba:

> The little house we live in now has no floor in it, but has quite a good chimney in so that I can cook a meal without smoking my eyes almost out of my head.

And John Brown, Jr.'s wife wrote to Mary Brown: "Our men have so much war and elections to attend to that it seems as though we were a great while getting into a house."

This is the manner in which the Brown families and almost all the Northern immigrants spent that desperate winter of 1855-56.

The tide began to shift against the South. More and more emigrants came from the North to settle the land and farm it, while in the main, Missourians came in for a day or two, raided, or dominated a political situation, and then went back to Missouri. The fact is that rather few pro-slavery men settled the land. As the tide against the South became more pronounced, shootings and killings became more frequent. There were killings in October and November. Then in late November, Lawrence, a stronghold of Free-State settlers, was threatened by destruction from pro-slavers, heavily augmented by Border Ruffians from Missouri. The Kansas Volunteers were called to defend the city. One of the companies which responded was the "Liberty Guards," headed by Captain John Brown, who had arrived but six weeks before. This is the first time the title of "Captain" was conferred upon him. In his company were four of his sons, John Brown, Jr., Salmon, Owen and Frederick.

There were long negotiations between the two armed camps. The Border Ruffians, realizing that Lawrence was well-defended, withdrew. Thus, Lawrence was saved. However, in January, 1856, President Pierce yielded to pro-slavery Governor Shannon and to Jefferson Davis (then Secretary of War, soon to become U.S. Senator for Mississippi, and later, President of the Confederacy), and proclaimed the Shawnee Legislature legal, stating that Free State men would be guilty of treason if they resisted by force. By declaring the Shawnee Legislature legal, President Pierce effectively denied Free Staters recourse to due process of law, because S. D. Lecompte, Chief Justice of Kansas Territory, and Judge Sterling G. Cato were both exceedingly strong pro-slavery men. Ralph Waldo Emerson, in a speech to aid Kansas delivered in Cambridge, Massachusetts on September 10, 1856, aptly summed up the situation:

> The Government armed and led the ruffians against the poor farmers. The judges give cowardly interpretations to the law. And of Kansas, the President says, "Let the complainant go to the courts;" though he knows that when the poor plundered farmer comes to the court, *he finds the ringleader who has robbed him dismounting his own horse, and unbuckling his knife to sit as his judge.*

Three weeks after his official proclamation recognizing the Shawnee Legislature, President Pierce placed the soldiers of Fort Riley and Fort Leavenworth at the disposal of Governor Shannon. In May, the pro-slavers, aided by Major Buford, who had come up with 400 to 500 men from Arkansas and Indian Territory [now Oklahoma], sacked Lawrence. The two anti-slavery newspapers were destroyed; their type and printing presses were thrown into the river. The Free State Hotel was fired on by pro-slavery cannon, then set ablaze and burned to the ground. Homes were ransacked and robbed.

The destruction of Lawrence took place on May 22, 1856. The Free Staters in the area had received a call to come to the aid of Lawrence. Thirty-four men from around Osawatomie and Pottawatomie responded, moving to Lawrence in a forced march. Among them were John Brown, five of his sons and his son-in-law, Henry Thompson. On the way to Lawrence, this group of 34 were stunned to learn that the town had already been taken and destroyed. They rested from their forced march that night. The following day, a council was held by about 15 of the 34, with John Brown as one of the spokesmen. John Brown said:

Now something must be done. We have got to defend our families and our neighbors as best we can. Something is going to be done now. We must show by actual work that there are two sides to this thing and that they cannot go on with impunity.

In later years, John Brown, Jr., recalling that day, May 23, 1856, wrote:

It was now and here resolved that they, their aiders and abettors, who sought to kill our suffering people, should themselves be killed, and in such a manner as should be likely to cause a restraining fear.

[48]

Salmon Brown, describing that same day, wrote:

The general purport of our intentions—some radical re-
taliatory measure—some killing—was well understood by the
whole camp. You never heard such cheering as they gave
us when we started out. They were wild with excitement
and enthusiasm. The principal man—the leader—in the
council that resolved on the necessity of Pottawatomie—was
H. H. Williams. He knew all those men on the Pottawatomie,
he lived among them—was familiar with their characters.
Not fifteen minutes before we left to go to Pottawatomie I
saw him, myself, write out a list of the men who were to be
killed and hand it to Father.

The band to do the killing was formed under John
Brown. It consisted of John Brown and seven men. Of the
seven, four were sons of John Brown—Salmon, Owen,
Frederick and Oliver. One was his son-in-law, Henry
Thompson, who, barely a month before this, on April 16,
had written to his wife:

It is a great trial to me to stay away from you, but I am
here, and feel I have a sacrifice to make, a duty to perform.
Can I leave that undone and feel easy, and have a conscience
void of offense? Should I ever feel that I have not put my
hand to the plough and looked back?

A month later, this man was to be involved in the five
killings on the Pottawatomie.

The eight men who were to do the killings rested in the
thickets all the day of the 24th, but they were not idle.
They sharpened and honed their short-bladed, heavy
swords to razor fineness. When full darkness enveloped
the night of May 24-25, the band marched toward
the home of their first victim, John Doyle. At about 11
o'clock that night, they knocked at his door, gained access
under point of rifle, took him and his two sons, William
and Drury, aged 22 and 20, into the thicket about 200

yards from the house, fell upon them and destroyed them. The next home to be visited was that of Allen Wilkinson, a member of the pro-slavery legislature. He, too, was killed in like manner; as spoils of war, his house was rifled of a gun, a powder flask and two saddles. The next to be killed was William Sherman; the spoils of war consisted of a horse and saddle. The killings were over.

We have a portrait of John Brown and his men during this period. James Redpath, who was to write the first book-length biography of John Brown, was at that time a correspondent for the *New York Tribune* and the *St. Louis Democrat*. He had lost his way in the woods and stumbled onto John Brown's camp on May 30, five days after the killings at Pottawatomie. Redpath describes the camp and its occupants:

Old Brown himself stood near the fire, with his shirt-sleeves rolled up, and a large piece of pork in his hand. He was cooking a pig. He was poorly clad, and his toes protruded from his boots. The old man received me with great cordiality, and the little band gathered about me.

In this camp no manner of profane language was permitted; no man of immoral character was allowed to stay, except as a prisoner of war. He made prayers in which all the company united, every morning and evening; and no food was ever tasted by his men until the Divine blessing had been asked on it. After every meal, thanks were returned to the Bountiful Giver.

It was at this time that the old man said to me: "I would rather have the small-pox, yellow fever, and cholera all together in my camp, than a man without principles. It's a mistake, sir," he continued, "that our people make, when they think that bullies are the best fighters, or that they are the men fit to oppose those Southerners. Give me men of good principles; God-fearing men; men who respect themselves; and, with a dozen of them, I will oppose any hundred such men as these Bufford ruffians."

I remained in the camp about an hour. Never before had I

met such a band of men. They were not earnest, but earnestness incarnate. Six of them were John Brown's sons.

The killing of the five men—the three Doyles, Wilkinson and Sherman—has evoked an enormous amount of literature by both the pro- and anti-John Brown camps. But I have never understood why this deed has been *especially* singled out from a long history of violence and suppression occasioned by slavery, a history of vigilantism and lynchings, when in border areas (and especially in Kansas Territory of 1854-59) the law was feebly and dishonestly enforced, and flouted more often than obeyed. Certainly, when examining the history and character structure of John Brown, this deed was a fairly direct and, to me, logical outcome of all that preceded. This Cromwellian, this Puritan with a strong touch of the idealism of the Transcendentalist, believed that he was acting in the name of God and of freedom.

Six years before, in 1850, while forming the League of the Gileadites, he had, as I have already noted, counseled the stringing up of slave catchers. Now, with the exacerbation of the slavery issue in Kansas Territory, he could not but believe that he was acting out of necessity, in accordance with his own teachings. The killings of Free Staters; the threats by pro-slavery and Missouri Border Ruffians to Northern settlers (who had traveled 1,500 and more miles to Kansas) to get out of the state within 48 hours on pain of being shot and their houses burned to the ground; the stuffing of ballot boxes in hundreds, even thousands, by Missourians; a pro-slavery legislature created by fraud and force; the denial of justice in courts officiated by rabid pro-slavery magistrates; the handing over by President Pierce of the entire machinery of government and the Federal armed forces of Fort Leavenworth and Fort Riley into the hands of the pro-slavery side—all this needed but one spark, the destruction of Lawrence, to start the conflagration.

[51]

John Brown, by temperament never a man to shirk responsibility or action, believing in the biblical injunction "an eye for an eye, a tooth for a tooth," led that band of eight who did the killings. Others in that group of 34, equally vociferous as to the need for the killings, prudently held back when the band under John Brown was formed— and one of those who held back was H. H. Williams, the very man who gave John Brown the execution list.

It was felt at that time by many in Kansas Territory that the important anti-slavery leaders were pleased by the killings; perhaps, even, that John Brown acted under their instruction, but that public policy forbade making this known. The thought here was that these violent killings would stay the hand of the pro-slavers and Border Ruffians.

I do not believe this; I do not believe John Brown took orders. The killings may have coincided with policy, but John Brown acted independently. He was never a man to take orders. I believe that he felt that if the Free Staters hadn't resisted, the probabilities are they would have been driven out of the Territory, which was the oft-stated intention of the pro-slavers. However, if John Brown thought to achieve a halt to the molestation of the Free Staters—a sort of paralysis because of the killings—then he failed in his purpose. A stalemate was achieved; a stalemate of terror and violence. Bands of men from both sides roamed the countryside. Houses were burned down. Smoking ruins became part of the landscape. Farms were abandoned. Scarcely a day went by without a skirmish or a fight. Shootings and burnings, capture and counter-capture of horses, cattle and equipment, were the order of the day.

John Brown's family suffered with the other Free Staters. At the Battle of Black Jack, one week after the killings at Pottawatomie, Henry Thompson was seriously wounded by enemy fire; Salmon Brown was also seriously wounded by the accidental discharge of a rifle. Two months later in Osawatomie, Frederick Brown, aged

26, was shot down and killed in cold blood one early morning when he went out to feed the horses. That same morning, Osawatomie was burned to the ground.

The burning of Osawatomie was part of an overall plan to rid Kansas Territory of Free Soilers. A force of 1,150 Border Ruffians, organized as a military brigade into two regiments, had extensive plans to attack the Free Soil towns, raiding and killing. In addition to Osawatomie, Topeka, Lawrence, Hickory Point and other settlements were to be set to the torch.

A force of 250 selected from the 1,150 Border Ruffians, surprised Osawatomie at dawn. John Brown rallied what force he could muster, about 45 men, and engaged in a defensive action while slowly retreating across the river. Young Luke Parsons reports the following conversation with John Brown just before going into battle:

"Parsons, were you ever under fire?" asked John Brown.

"No, but I will obey orders. Tell me what you want me to do," said Parsons.

"Take more care to end life well than to live long," counseled John Brown.

The defense was overwhelmed. The Border Ruffians quickly gained control of the settlement, took horses and cattle, looted the 25 houses and stores, and then set fire to the buildings. Jason Brown, on the other side of the river with his father, described the tears coursing down John Brown's cheeks. As they watched the consuming flames, John Brown cried out:

God sees it. I have only a short time to live—only one death to die, and I will die fighting for this cause. There will be no more peace in this land until slavery is done for. I will give them something else to do than to extend slave territory. I will carry the war into Africa.

The father and son stood together for a time, watching the burning of Osawatomie. Then, they crossed the river at a safer point to search for Frederick Brown's body.

[53]

The man who shot Frederick Brown that early morning was The Reverend Martin White, a pro-slaver whose home was in Missouri, and who had joined the Border Ruffians. Two years to the very month after the killing of Frederick, when John Brown was back again in Kansas, he made a scouting expedition into Missouri. He and his group of three men came on a hill and there below them was The Reverend Martin White's house. Eli Snyder, one of the three men, relates how he looked through the field glass they had with them:

Looking I could recognize Martin White reading a book as he sat in a chair in the shade of a tree. I handed the glass to Brown and asked him to look and he said he also recognized him saying: "I declare that is Martin White." For a few minutes nothing was said when I remarked, "Suppose you and I go down and see the old man and have a talk with him." "No, no, I can't do that," said Brown. Kagi [who was to be John Brown's second in command at Harpers Ferry] said, "Let Snyder and me go." Captain Brown said: "Go if you wish to but don't you hurt a hair of his head; but if he has any slaves take the last one of them." Kagi said: "Snyder and I want to go without instructions, or not at all." Therefore as Brown was unwilling that Martin White, who had murdered his son, should receive any harm we did not go near him.

At a later time John Brown said about The Reverend Martin White:

I would not hurt one hair of his head. I would not go one inch to take his life; I do not harbour the feelings of revenge. *I act from a principle.* My aim and object is to restore human rights.

I have described James Redpath's portrait of John Brown when he stumbled onto his camp, five days after the Pottawatomie killings. We are fortunate to have still

[54]

another interesting portrait of the John Brown of this period.

William A. Phillips, a lawyer from Illinois, went to Kansas at the age of 31, and there served as correspondent for the *New York Tribune*. After the Civil War, during which time he had been an officer in the Union army, he became an editor, and also was elected to Congress for three terms. *The Atlantic Monthly* for December, 1879, published an article by Phillips recounting three interviews he had with John Brown; this article is reprinted in its entirety in Louis Ruchames's *A John Brown Reader*. The first of these took place on July 2, a little more than a month after Pottawatomie.

The Free State Legislature had arranged to assemble in Topeka. The pro-slavery party, aided by Border Ruffians who had come in from Missouri, plus the military forces of the Federal Government which had been handed over to the pro-slavery party by President Pierce, firmly intended to prevent such a meeting. It was expected that anywhere up to 1,000 Free Soil men would converge on Topeka to defend the meeting of the Free State Legislature. John Brown, with a band of 22 men under his command, was proceeding to Topeka to aid in the defense. On the way, he stopped off in Lawrence and called on Phillips. Since Phillips was also going to Topeka, he joined Brown and his band of 22; together they journeyed to Topeka. Phillips wrote of this meeting and journey:

I had my first good opportunity to judge the old man's character. I had seen him in his camp, had seen him in the field, and he was always an enigma, a strange compound of enthusiasm and cold, methodic stolidity—a volcano beneath a mountain of snow.

We placed our two saddles together, so that our heads lay only a few feet apart. It was past eleven o'clock, and we lay there until two in the morning, scarcely time enough for sleep; indeed, we slept none. He seemed to be as little disposed to sleep as I was, and we talked; or rather he did, for I said little more than enough to keep him going. I soon found that he was a very thorough astronomer, and he enlightened me on a good many matters in the starry firmament above us. He pointed out the different constellations and their movements. "Now," he said, "it is midnight," and he pointed to the finger marks of his great clock in the sky.

In his ordinary moods the man seemed so rigid, stern, and unimpressible when I first knew him that I never thought a poetic and impulsive nature lay behind that cold exterior. The whispering of the wind on the prairie was full of voices to him, and the stars as they shone in the firmament of God seemed to inspire him. "How admirable is the symmetry of the heavens; how grand and beautiful. Everything moves in sublime harmony in the government of God. Not so with us poor creatures."

Of the pro-slavery men he spoke in bitterness. He said that slavery besotted everything, and made men more brutal and coarse. Nor did the freestate men escape his sharp censure. He said that we had many noble and true men, but that we had too many broken-down politicians from the older States. These men, he said, would rather pass resolutions than act, and they criticised all who did real work. A professional politician, he went on, you never could trust; for even if he had convictions, he was always ready to sacrifice his principles for his advantage.

One of the most interesting things in his conversation that night, and one that marked him as a theorist (and perhaps to some extent he might be styled a visionary), was his treatment of our forms of social and political life. He thought society ought to be organized on a less selfish basis; for while material interests gained something by the deification of pure selfishness, men and women lost much by it. He said that all great reforms, like the Christian religion, were based on broad, generous, self-sacrificing principles. He condemned the sale of land as a chattel, and thought that there was an infinite number of wrongs to right before society would be what it should be, but that in our country slavery was the "sum of all villainies," and its abolition the first

[56]

essential work. If the American people did not take courage and end it speedily, human freedom and republican liberty would soon be empty names in these United States.

The dew lay cold and heavy on the grass and on the blanket above us. My companion paused for a short time, and I thought he was going to sleep, when he said, "It is nearly two o'clock, and as it must be nine or ten miles to Topeka it is time we were marching," and again he drew my attention to his index marks in the sky. He rose and called his men. In less than ten minutes the company had saddled, packed, and mounted, and was again on the march.

Early in September, 1856, John W. Geary took office as the new Governor of Kansas Territory. The pressures of Free State settlers were such that Geary realized the political necessity of enforcing the law impartially; he ordered the disbandment of all extra-military companies and guerrilla bands. Slowly, very slowly, order began to emerge out of chaos.

As for John Brown and his family, Oliver, Salmon, and Henry Thompson started north for Iowa in August; John Brown, John Brown, Jr., Jason and Owen headed north in October. As I have said, Henry Thompson was badly injured; so was Salmon Brown. The other sons of John Brown, suffering from chills and fever, were thin and debilitated. John Brown himself was in such poor condition that he had to lie on a pallet in the carriage. Frederick was dead, shot down in cold blood by Reverend Martin White. John Brown and his family had paid a heavy price fighting against slavery that year in Kansas.

* * * * * *

While in Kansas, during November, 1855, John Brown had written to his wife:

I think much, too, of your kind of widowed state; and I

[57]

sometimes allow myself to dream a little of again some time enjoying the comforts of home, but I do not dare to dream much. May God abundantly reward all your sacrifices for humanity.

Indeed, as we shall see, he did not allow himself much time to enjoy the comforts of home and wife.

From Kansas, John Brown journeyed East. He arrived late in December, 1856, after being away from home and family for a year and a half. His first stop was at the home of Frederick Douglass—of whom I shall speak in some detail shortly. John Brown stayed at Douglass's house for several days and then went to Boston. He spoke there and in other New England communities in order to recruit men and money for Kansas.

In New England during the early part of 1857, he met many of the leading Transcendentalists, and also many of the most intense abolitionists: Judge Thomas Russell, Ralph Waldo Emerson, Henry Thoreau, William Lloyd Garrison, Wendell Phillips, Amos Lawrence. But more important than any of these, were the six men who became John Brown's principal New England supporters: Gerrit Smith, member of Congress, millionaire, philanthropist; Reverend Theodore Parker, Unitarian minister, orator, master of 20 languages, owner of a library of 16,000 volumes; Frank B. Sanborn, educator, teacher, and, in later years, a biographer of John Brown; Dr. Samuel G. Howe, physician, who had fought both with Garibaldi and for Greek independence, and who was founder of the Massachusetts School for the Blind, and with his wife, Julia Ward Howe, was co-editor of an abolitionist paper; George Luther Stearns, wealthy merchant and philanthropist; Reverend Thomas Wentworth Higginson, fiery Unitarian minister of Worcester, (as a colonel during the Civil War, Higginson led the first black regiment formed, the First South Carolina Volunteers, a regiment which consisted of freed slaves; subsequently he wrote his *Army Life In A Black Regiment*, recently republished). In later years, these men were referred to as the Secret Six.

When John Brown spoke in Town Hall, Concord, in 1857, Emerson recorded the following in his diary:

Captain John Brown gave a good account of himself in the Town Hall last night. One of his good points was the folly of the peace party in Kansas, who believed that their strength lay in the greatness of their wrongs, and so discountenanced resistance. He wished to know if their wrong was greater than the negro's, and what kind of strength that gave to the negro?

And Thoreau, speaking about him said:

I should say that he is an old-fashioned man in his respect for the Constitution, and his faith in the permanence of this Union. Slavery he deems to be wholly opposed to these, and he is a determined foe. A man of rare commonsense and directness of speech, as of action; a transcendentalist above all, a man of ideas and principles,—that is what distinguishes him. I noticed that he did not overstate anything, but spoke within bounds. In his speech here, he referred to what his family had suffered in Kansas, without ever giving the least vent to his pent-up fire. It was a volcano with an ordinary chimney-flue.

On February 19, 1857, John Brown appeared before a Joint Committee of the Massachusetts Legislature, then considering an appropriation in aid of Kansas. We can see the kind of speech Thoreau had in mind when he described John Brown as "a volcano with an ordinary chimney-flue." Relating his experience in Kansas to the Joint Committee, John Brown said:

I once saw three mangled bodies, two of which were dead, and one alive, but with twenty bullet and buck shot holes in him, after the two murdered men had lain on the ground, to be worked at by flies, for some eighteen hours. One of these young men was my own son.

[59]

Some of his listeners learned for the first time, while others had driven home to them with renewed force, the necessity under certain conditions to transform a doctrine into a deed. Certainly his work in Kansas and his talks in Boston, Concord, Hartford, New Haven, Worcester, Springfield and several other places, influenced the thinking of a host of intellectual and spiritual leaders in New England.

In all, John Brown was in the New England area for four months, speaking and conferring from January through April, before he journeyed to his home and family in North Elba. He had been away for 21 months; he stayed for 12 days. On the thirteenth day, he set out on his second journey to Kansas Territory. Once again, his wife was to be reduced to a "kind of widowed state."

*　*　*　*　*　*

John Brown returned to Kansas during November, 1857. He stayed but a few weeks. He was not engaged in battle; there was no violence. The new governor had pledged himself to maintain honesty at the polls and was prepared to call out the military if necessary to honor his pledge. By this time there was large-scale permanent migration from the North, as compared to the dwindling numbers coming from the South. Thus the North had every expectation of achieving victory by ballot, rather than by bullet.

John Brown was not idle during his second stay in Kansas. He was busy recruiting the core of his men who were to serve with him to the end—at Harpers Ferry. He took these men to Springdale, a remote town in Iowa, where many Quaker abolitionists had settled. There the men spent the next several months, training and drilling. Having settled the men in Springdale, John Brown traveled east to Rochester, New York, where late in January, 1858, he knocked for a second time at Frederick Douglass's door.

Frederick Douglass was then 41 years old. Twenty years before, he had escaped from the South. He was a man of extraordinary capacity. Within a half-year after his escape, he was a speaker at a public meeting. Two years later, at the age of 24, he became a lecturer for the Massachusetts Anti-Slavery Society, thus launching a long career in public life.

Frederick Douglass, a man of imposing physical presence, was a superb writer and a brilliant orator. He was also a man of great personal courage. Many a time he was forced to slip out the back door of a lecture hall and into a waiting carriage, in order to escape attack by proslavery mobs. He was mauled and roughly handled more than once. Often, refused the hire of a hall, he would call his meeting in an open field or wood, where there was no back door. In 1848, in Pendleton, Indiana, while on a lecture tour for the New England Anti-Slavery Society, he held such an open-air meeting and was set upon by a mob. His right hand was broken and he was knocked unconscious.

He fought segregation in public conveyances vigorously, often at the cost of a beating. He describes such an experience:

I made it a rule to seat myself in the cars for the accommodation of passengers generally. Thus seated, I was sure to be called upon to betake myself to the "Jim Crow car." Refusing to obey, I was often dragged out of my seat, beaten, and severely bruised, by conductors and trainmen. Attempting to start from Lynn one day, I went, as my custom was, into one of the best railroad carriages on the road. I was soon visited by half a dozen fellows of the baser sort, and told that I must move out of that seat, and if I did not, they would drag me out. I refused to move, and they clutched me, head, neck, and shoulders. But, in anticipation of the stretching to which I was about to be subjected, I had interwoven myself among the seats. In dragging me out, on this occasion, it must have cost the company twenty-five or thirty dollars, for I tore up seats and all. So great was the excitement in Lynn, on the subject, that the superintendent ordered trains to run through Lynn without stopping, while I remained in the town; and this ridiculous farce was enacted. For several days the trains went dashing through Lynn without stopping.

In 1845, to refute the charge that he could not possibly have been a slave, for no slave could write and speak so superbly, he published the first of his three autobiographies, *Narrative of the Life of Frederick Douglass*. In it he mentioned specific names, places and dates of his boyhood, proving conclusively he *had* been a slave. The contention that no slave could achieve Douglass's level stemmed from the South's need to justify its ideological position that slaves were not human beings; that they were a subspecies, not quite beast, but not quite man. Therefore, it was permissible to own them, to buy and sell them for profit, treat them as one treats a horse or cow. But if a slave, only several years out of slavery and largely self-taught, could accomplish what Frederick Douglass did, then this aspect of the argument had no basis.

Frederick Douglass knew before his book was published that by naming names, places and dates, he ran the risk of being apprehended by slave catchers and returned to his owner. He took that risk.

He became free of this danger in the late part of 1846. He had traveled to England, Ireland, and Scotland, and lectured against slavery with tremendous success. His British friends purchased his freedom for $710.96 and presented him with the bill of sale. Writing about this, he said:

I am indebted not to democratic humanity or justice for the liberty I have enjoyed—but to humane British men and women who bought my body and bones with British gold, and made me a present to myself. In other words, they gave me back the body originally given me by my Creator, but which had been stolen from me under the singularly just and generous laws of a republican slave State!

In 1855, he published his second book, *My Bondage and My Freedom*. These two books evoked enormous furor in pre-Civil War time; to this day, they are of abiding interest. His third book, *The Life and Times of Frederick Douglass*, published in 1881, toward the end of his life, is of huge scope.

Frederick Douglass poured forth a constant cascade of magnificent speeches and articles on the issue of the day. Often, with ironic precision, yet suffused with great passion, he exposed the vast gulf that existed between the pretension and the fact. Here he is, in 1852, addressing a white audience at a July Fourth celebration in Rochester, New York:

Why am I called upon to speak here today? What have I, or those I represent, to do with your national independence? Are the principles of political freedom and of natural justice, embodied in the Declaration of Independence, extended to us?

The blessings in which you, this day, rejoice, are not enjoyed in common. The rich inheritance of justice, liberty, prosperity and independence, bequeathed by your fathers, is shared by you, not by me. The sunlight that brought light and healing to you, has brought stripes and death to me. This Fourth July is *yours*, not *mine*. *You* may rejoice, *I* must mourn. To drag a man in fetters into the grand illuminated temple of liberty, and call upon him to join you in joyous anthems, were inhuman mockery and sacrilegious irony. Do you mean, citizens, to mock me by asking me to speak to-day?

What, to the American slave is your 4th of July? I answer; a day that reveals to him, more than all other days in the year, the gross injustice and cruelty to which he is the constant victim. To him, your celebration is a sham; your boasted liberty, an unholy license; your national greatness, swelling vanity; your sounds of rejoicing are empty and heartless; your denunciation of tyrants, brass fronted impudence; your shouts of liberty and equality, hollow mockery; your prayers and hymns, your sermons and thanksgivings, with all your religious parade and solemnity, are, to him, mere bombast, fraud, deception, impiety and hyprocrisy —a thin veil to cover up crimes which would disgrace a nation of savages.

Americans! your republican politics, not less than your republican religion, are flagrantly inconsistent. You boast of your love of liberty, your superior civilization, and your pure Christianity, while the whole political power of the nation (as embodied in the two great political parties) is solemnly pledged to support the enslavement of three million of your countrymen. You profess to believe "That, of one blood, God made all nations of men to dwell on the face of all the earth," and hath commanded all men, everywhere, to love one another; yet you notoriously hate (and glory in your hatred) all men whose skins are not colored like your own.

The existence of slavery in this country brands your republicanism as a sham, your humanity as a base pretence, and your Christianity as a lie. It destroys your moral power abroad; it corrupts your politicians at home. It saps the foundation of religion; it makes your name a hissing and a bye-word to a mocking earth. It is the antagonistic force in your government, the only thing that seriously disturbs and endangers your *Union*.

Although Douglass was mainly concerned with the central issue of freedom for slaves, he did not give freedom a narrow interpretation. He participated in all the struggles of the period. To cite but one example: in 1848, at Seneca Falls, New York, he attended the first Women's Rights Convention ever held anywhere in the world. When Elizabeth Cady Stanton proposed the motion that women shall have the right of suffrage, Frederick Douglass was the one to second the motion.

Frederick Douglass founded his newspaper, *The North*

[64]

Star, in 1847, the first issue of which was published in December. During that month, John Brown and Frederick Douglass met in Springfield, Massachusetts, where John Brown, trying to repair his fortunes, was in the wool business with a partner. Douglass described John Brown as a man who "Though a white gentleman, is in sympathy a black man, and is deeply interested in our cause, as though his own soul had been pressed with the iron of slavery."

John Brown invited Douglass to his house and Douglass spent a night and a day there. Here he describes his first meal at John Brown's house:

> It consisted of beef soup, cabbage and potatoes, a meal such as a man might relish after following the plough all day. There were no hired help visible. The mother, daughters and sons did the serving, and did it well. It is said that a house in some measure reflects the character of its occupants; this one certainly did. In it there were no disguises, no illusions, no make-believes; everything implied stern truth, solid purpose, and rigid economy.

I have said that in 1841 Frederick Douglass was engaged by the Massachusetts Anti-Slavery Society to lecture for them. This organization took its platform from William Lloyd Garrison and his anti-slavery paper, *The Liberator.* One of the important tenets of the Garrisonian abolitionists was that moral suasion would be the means of ending slavery, that even the slaveholder ultimately convinced of the sin of slavery would be voluntarily converted and turn from it. In a speech at that time, Douglas said: "It is the moral movement, the appeal to men's sense of right, which makes them and all our opponents tremble."

When Douglass met John Brown in 1847, he was still a Garrisonian abolitionist preaching moral suasion and voluntary conversion. Douglass was in for a surprise. When the first meal that Douglass had with John Brown and his family was over, the two men talked. He learned from John Brown that:

He thought that slaveholders had forfeited their right to live; that the slaves had the right to gain their liberty in any way they could; did not believe that moral suasion would ever liberate the slave.

Then, after cautiously sounding out Douglass, John Brown revealed his plan:

He called my attention to a map of the United States, and pointed out to me the far-reaching Alleghanies, which stretch away from the borders of New York into the Southern states.

"These mountains", he said, "are the basis of my plan. God has given the strength of the hills to freedom; they were placed here for the emancipation of the Negro race; they are full of natural forts, where one man for defense will be equal to a hundred for attack; they are full also of good hiding-places, where large numbers of brave men could be concealed, and baffle and elude pursuit for a long time. I know these mountains well, and could take a body of men into them and keep them there despite of all efforts of Virginia to dislodge them. The true object to be sought is first of all to destroy the money value of slavery property; and that can only be done by rendering such property insecure. My plan, then, is to take at first about twenty-five picked men, and begin on a small scale; supply them with arms and ammunition and post them in squads of fives on a line of twenty-five miles. The most persuasive and judicious of these shall go down to the fields from time to time, as opportunity offers, and induce the slaves to join them; seeking and selecting the most restless and daring."

With care and enterprise he thought he could soon gather a force of one hundred hardy men; when these were properly drilled, they would run off the slaves in large numbers, retain the brave and strong ones in the mountains and send the weak and timid to the North by the Underground Railroad. His operations would be enlarged with increasing numbers and would not be confined to one locality.

When I asked him how he would support these men, he said

[66]

emphatically that he would subsist them upon the enemy. Slavery was a state of war and the slave had a right to anything necessary to his freedom. "But", said I, "suppose you succeed in running off a few slaves, and thus impress the Virginia slaveholders with a sense of insecurity in their slaves,—the effect will only be to make them sell their slaves further south." "That", he said, "will be what I want first to do; then I would follow them up. If we could drive slavery out of one county, it would be a great gain; it would weaken the system throughout the state."

Douglass, the proponent of moral suasion, found himself confronted by an advocate of direct action. John Brown's conviction that slavery was a state of war demanding military interference had a profound effect upon Douglass. Writing about that evening, he said:

From this night spent with John Brown in Springfield, Massachusetts, 1847, while I continued to write and speak against slavery, I became all the same less hopeful of its peaceful abolition. My utterances became more and more tinged by the color of this man's strong impressions.

They became trusting friends and when John Brown knocked at Frederick Douglass's door in Rochester in January, 1858, saying it was commonly thought he was still in Kansas Territory and therefore must keep his whereabouts secret, Douglass immediately made arrangements for him to stay. John Brown said, "I will not stay unless you allow me to pay board." Douglass charged John Brown three dollars a week. John Brown stayed for about three weeks.

Within a day or two after his arrival, John Brown wrote home to North Elba to let his family know he was out of Kansas Territory and safe:

I am (praised be God!) once more in New York State. Whether or not I shall be permitted to visit you or not this winter or spring, I cannot now say; but it is some relief of mind to feel that I am again so near you. Possibly if I cannot go to see you, I may be able to devise some way for one or more of you to meet me somewhere. The anxiety I feel to see my wife and children once more I am unable to describe. The cries of my poor sorrow-stricken despairing children, whose "tears on their cheeks" are ever in my eyes, and whose sighs are ever in my ears, may however prevent my enjoying the happiness I so much desire. But, courage, courage, courage! the great work of my life I may yet see accomplished (God helping), and be permitted to return, and "rest at evening."

A week later he writes to John Brown, Jr., instructing him to make a trip to Bedford, Chambersburg, Gettysburg and Uniontown, to find families "of the right stripe" and get to know them as much as he could. For, "when you look at the location of those places, you will readily perceive the advantage of getting up some acquaintance in these parts." And, indeed, a study of the map will show that John Brown was desirous of locating anti-slavery families in order to learn the stations along the Underground from Harpers Ferry into the Pennsylvania section of the Alleghenies to facilitate moving men and materials back and forth as needed.

But for the most part, he was busy writing to wealthy Northern abolitionists and other anti-slavery people; a campaign to get support and money. Until the end, he was never free of the burden of raising money. The total sum John Brown raised from this time until the raid on Harpers Ferry was in the neighborhood of $2,500.

In addition to letter-writing, John Brown was, as Douglass wrote, engaged in:

writing and revising a constitution, which he meant to put in operation by the men who should go with him in the Virginia mountains. He said that to avoid anarchy and confusion, there should be a regularly constituted government, which each man who came with him should be sworn to honor and support.

[68]

Frederick Douglass in middle age.

Frederick Douglass

NARRATIVE

OF THE

LIFE

OF

FREDERICK DOUGLASS,

AN

AMERICAN SLAVE.

WRITTEN BY HIMSELF.

BOSTON:

PUBLISHED AT THE ANTI-SLAVERY OFFICE,

No. 25 CORNHILL

1845.

Fred^k. Douglass.

LIFE AND TIMES

OF

FREDERICK DOUGLASS,

WRITTEN BY HIMSELF.

HIS EARLY LIFE AS A SLAVE, HIS ESCAPE FROM BONDAGE,

AND HIS COMPLETE HISTORY

TO THE

PRESENT TIME

INCLUDING HIS CONNECTION WITH THE ANTI-SLAVERY MOVEMENT ; HIS LABORS IN GREAT
BRITAIN AS WELL AS IN HIS OWN COUNTRY ; HIS EXPERIENCE IN THE CONDUCT OF
AN INFLUENTIAL NEWSPAPER ; HIS CONNECTION WITH THE UNDERGROUND
RAILROAD ; HIS RELATIONS WITH JOHN BROWN AND THE HARPER'S
FERRY RAID ; HIS RECRUITING THE 54th AND 55th MASS.
COLORED REGIMENTS ; HIS INTERVIEWS WITH
PRESIDENTS LINCOLN AND JOHNSON ;
HIS APPOINTMENT BY GEN. GRANT TO ACCOMPANY THE SANTO DOMINGO COMMISSION ; ALSO
TO A SEAT IN THE COUNCIL OF THE DISTRICT OF COLUMBIA ; HIS APPOINTMENT AS
UNITED STATES MARSHAL BY PRESIDENT R. B. HAYES ; ALSO HIS APPOINTMENT
BY PRESIDENT J. A. GARFIELD TO BE RECORDER OF DEEDS IN
WASHINGTON ; WITH MANY OTHER INTERESTING AND
IMPORTANT EVENTS OF HIS MOST
EVENTFUL LIFE ;

WITH AN INTRODUCTION,

BY MR. GEORGE L. RUFFIN,

OF BOSTON

HARTFORD, CONN.:
PARK PUBLISHING CO.
1881.

Harriet Tubman had a price of $40,000 on her head. (Library of Congress, Prints and Photographs.)

SCENES

IN THE LIFE OF

HARRIET TUBMAN

BY

SARAH H. BRADFORD.

AUBURN:
W. J. MOSES, PRINTER.
1869.

THE

UNDERGROUND RAIL ROAD.

A RECORD

OF

Facts, Authentic Narratives, Letters, &c.,

Narrating the Hardships Hair-breadth Escapes and Death Struggles

OF THE

Slaves in their efforts for Freedom,

AS RELATED

BY THEMSELVES AND OTHERS, OR WITNESSED BY THE AUTHOR;

TOGETHER WITH

SKETCHES OF SOME OF THE LARGEST STOCKHOLDERS, AND

MOST LIBERAL AIDERS AND ADVISERS,

OF THE ROAD.

BY

WILLIAM STILL,

For many years connected with the Anti-Slavery Office in Philadelphia, and Chairman
of the Acting Vigilant Committee of the Philadelphia Branch of
the Underground Rail Road.

Illustrated with 70 fine Engravings by Bensell, Schell and others, and
Portraits from Photographs from Life.

———————

Thou shalt not deliver unto his master the servant that has escaped from his master unto thee.—*Deut.* xxiii. 15.

———————

SOLD ONLY BY SUBSCRIPTION.

PHILADELPHIA:
PORTER & COATES,
822, CHESTNUT STREET.
1872.

Four "Conductors" of the Underground Railroad: Samuel D. Burris, Abigail Goodwin, J. Miller McKim, William Whipper.

CAUTION!!

COLORED PEOPLE

OF BOSTON, ONE & ALL,

You are hereby respectfully CAUTIONED and advised, to avoid conversing with the

Watchmen and Police Officers of Boston,

For since the recent ORDER OF THE MAYOR & ALDERMEN, they are empowered to act as

KIDNAPPERS
AND
Slave Catchers,

And they have already been actually employed in KIDNAPPING, CATCHING, AND KEEPING SLAVES. Therefore, if you value your LIBERTY, and the *Welfare of the Fugitives* among you, *Shun* them in every possible manner, as so many *HOUNDS* on the track of the most unfortunate of your race.

Keep a Sharp Look Out for KIDNAPPERS, and have TOP EYE open.

APRIL 24, 1851.

After the passage of the Fugitive Slave Law posters such as this began to appear in the North. (From the New York Public Library, Schomburg Collection.)

This constitution which John Brown was working on was, as we shall soon see, the Provisional Constitution of the Chatham Convention.

From Rochester he went to Peterboro, New York, to the home of Gerrit Smith. There he discussed his plan with several people, among them, Frank Sanborn. Sanborn, upon hearing John Brown's plan, was tempted to cast his lot with him, but he held back because of other ties and calls. John Brown writes to him a few days after their discussion:

Mr. Norton has taken the liberty of saying to me that you felt half inclined to make a common cause with me. I greatly rejoice at this; for I believe when you come to look at the ample field I labor in, and the rich harvest which not only this entire country but the whole world during the present and future generations may reap from its successful cultivation, you will feel that you are out of your element until you find you are in it, an entire unit. What an inconceivable amount of good you might so effect by your counsel, your example, your encouragement, your natural and acquired ability for active service! And then, how very little we can possibly lose! I have only had this one opportunity, in a life of nearly sixty years; and could I be continued ten times as long again, I might not again have another equal opportunity. God has honored but comparatively a very small part of mankind with any possible chance for such mighty and soul-satisfying rewards. But, my dear friend, if you should make up your mind to do so, I trust it will be wholly from the promptings of your own spirit, after having thoroughly counted the cost. I would flatter no man into such a measure, if I could do it ever so easily.

I expect nothing but to "endure hardness;" but I expect to effect a mighty conquest, even though it be like the last victory of Samson. I felt for a number of years, in earlier life, a steady, strong desire to die; but since I saw any prospect of becoming a "reaper" in the great harvest, I have not only felt quite willing to live, but have enjoyed life much; and am now rather anxious to live for a few years more.

A month later, in Boston trying to raise funds, John Brown met with the Unitarian minister, Reverend Thomas Wentworth Higginson. Here is Higginson's description of John Brown:

> On his thin, worn, resolute face there were the signs of a fire which might wear him out, and practically did so, but nothing of pettiness or baseness; and his talk was calm, persuasive, and coherent. He was simply a high-minded, unselfish, belated Covenanter; a man whom Sir Walter Scott might have drawn. He had that religious elevation which is itself a kind of refinement; the quality one may see expressed in many a venerable Quaker face at yearly meeting.

While in Boston, John Brown wrote to John Brown, Jr., again alerting him to the need of finding friends "of the right stripe" along the route to the South as quickly as possible. This time there was specific mention of Harpers Ferry: "As it may require sometime to hunt out friends at Bedford, Chambersburg, Gettysburg, Hagerstown, Maryland, or even *Harper's Ferry, Virginia,* I would like to have you arrange your business so as to set out very soon."

Two days later, he writes once more to John Brown, Jr., requesting that he come to Philadelphia to attend a meeting to be held in the house of The Reverend Stephen Smith. At the meeting, in addition to John Brown and John Brown, Jr., were Frederick Douglass, The Reverend Henry Highland Garnet, William Still and probably several others. Except for John Brown and his son, all were Negroes.

The Reverend Henry Highland Garnet was the grandson of an African chief and a militant abolitionist. At a National Negro Convention in Buffalo in 1843, Garnet, then 27 years old, delivered a clarion-call speech to the more than 70 delegates present from many states in the Union, wherein he concluded with:

[70]

Brethren, arise, arise! Strike for your lives and liberties. Now is the day and the hour. Let every slave throughout the land do this, and the days of slavery are numbered. You cannot be more oppressed than you have been—you cannot suffer greater cruelties than you have already. *Rather die freemen than live to be slaves.* Remember that you are FOUR MILLIONS! Heaven, as with a voice of thunder, calls on you to arise from the dust. Let your motto be resistance! *Resistance!* RESISTANCE! No oppressed people have ever secured their liberty without resistance.

At this convention, Frederick Douglass had opposed Henry Highland Garnet, calling for moral suasion and nonviolent resistance. The way to abolish slavery was to set up "in the hearts of men a deep and wide-spreading connection of the brotherhood of the human race; that God hath indeed made of one blood all nations of men for to dwell on all the face of the earth." Garnet's militant position was defeated, Douglass's position of moral suasion winning by one vote. Now 15 years later, these two were in the same room committed to an activist policy.

For John Brown, however, the most important man at this meeting was William Still, "conductor" of the Underground Railroad Station of Philadelphia. During the course of Still's work, he had received literally thousands of fugitives from stations south of Philadelphia and passed them along to stations further north. The men in this room had accumulated a great mass of information from refugee slaves regarding routes and places to hide, which they gave to John Brown and his son.

Shortly after the Philadelphia meeting, the two John Browns went to Frederick Douglass's home in Rochester. There they separated, with the older John Brown going up to St. Catherine's, in West Canada, where, early in April, 1858, he met with Harriet Tubman. An escaped slave, she had made 19 trips back into the South and had led to Canada and freedom over 300 slaves without losing a single one of her charges, thereby earning the appellation, "Moses of her People." With each successful foray the price for her capture rose, so that ultimately she had the incredible price of $40,000 on her head, dead or alive.

By 1858, there were about 40,000 Negroes living in West Canada. There had been race riots in Cincinnati, Ohio, in 1829. Blacks had been shot down in the streets and in their homes. When the governor of West Canada invited the Negroes of Cincinnati to settle there, about 1,000 migrated across the border. They formed their own community, Wilberforce Settlement, close to London, Ontario, and established Wilberforce Institute, a school for the education and training of Negroes. However, most of the blacks in West Canada were slaves who had escaped via the Underground Railroad and were now living under the British flag. A rising number, trained at Wilberforce, were mechanics, merchants and farmers. Doctors, lawyers and other professional men began to make their appearance. More than a few had begun to accumulate wealth. Harriet Tubman agreed to recruit soldiers for John Brown from this community of blacks. Later, when his plan had been put into effect, she would be his chief guide.

On April 8, John Brown writes with guarded jubilation to John Brown, Jr.:

I am succeeding, to all appearances, beyond my expectations. Harriet Tubman hooked on his whole team at once. He (Harriet) is the most of a man, naturally, that I ever met with. There is the most abundant material, and of the right quality, in this quarter, beyond all doubt. Do not forget to write Mr. Case (near Rochester) at once about hunting up every person and family of the reliable kind about at, or near Bedford, Chambersburg, Gettysburg, and Carlisle, in Pennsylvania, and also Hagerstown and vicinity, Maryland, and *Harpers Ferry, Virginia.*

At that same time, April, 1858, John Brown approached black leaders of West Canada, acquainted them in part with his plan, and with them worked out details for the Chatham Convention. Directly after that he went back to Springdale, Iowa, to pick up the men he had left there to train and drill, and brought them back to Chatham for the Convention, which took place from May 8 to May 10.

There were 46 attending the Chatham Convention: 34 Negroes, John Brown, and the 11 men he had brought up from Springdale. To divert suspicion, it was given out that the convention was called to form an organization of Negro Masons.

The Chatham Convention can be understood only within the framework of John Brown's larger design. He planned to go into the Southern mountain ranges of the Alleghenies, capture sections of it, and set up an independent government. It was the function of the Chatham Convention to adopt a Provisional Constitution for the territory captured, elect the officers, and, in general, to have the administrative machinery of government ready when needed. Hostilities would cease only when the individual states and the United States Government agreed to abolish slavery.

Let us now examine the Provisional Constitution that emanated from the Chatham Convention. The text of this Provisional Constitution can be found in Richard J. Hinton's *John Brown and His Men.* We shall see that its structure is loosely modeled after our Federal Constitution, but with numerous modifications applicable to a band of guerrillas. First, the preamble:

Whereas slavery, throughout its entire existence in the United States, is none other than a most barbarous, unprovoked, and unjustifiable war of one portion of its citizens upon another portion, the only conditions of which are perpetual imprisonment and hopeless servitude or absolute extermination; in utter disregard and violation of those eternal and self-evident truths set forth in our Declaration of Independence; Therefore

We, citizens of the United States, and the Oppressed Peo-

[73]

ple, who, by a recent decision of the Supreme Court are declared to have no rights which the White Man is bound to respect; together with all other people degraded by the laws thereof, Do, for the time being ordain and establish ourselves, the following PROVISIONAL CONSTITUTION AND ORDINANCES, the better to protect our Persons, Property, Lives, and Liberties; and to govern our actions.

This preamble stated formally what John Brown had said to Frederick Douglass at their first meeting, namely, that slavery was a state of war. Slavery was institutionalized violence, sanctioned by a government controlled by the slaveowning powers. Slavery owed its existence to the superior force which a more powerful section of the people exercised upon a weaker, defenseless portion. Slaves, therefore, were prisoners of war; John Brown proposed to free these prisoners of war. In short, the preamble stated an ideological premise from which flowed the constitution and its justification.

The body of the Provisional Constitution consists of 48 articles. The first group details the establishment of the legislative, executive and judicial branches, the judiciary being independent of the other two. Provisions were made for a president, vice-president, unicameral congress, supreme court, secretaries of war, state and treasury and a commander-in-chief; their duties were detailed.

Some of the other articles bear examination:

> All captured or confiscated property, and all property the product of the labor of those belonging to this organization and of their families, shall be held as the property of the whole, equally, without distinction; and may be used for the common benefit.

John Brown envisaged a communal form of government. It must be borne in mind that at this time a number of communal societies had been established in the United States: Oneida Community, the Shakers, Brook

[74]

Farm, the Amonites, New Harmony. In the communal society to be established by the Provisional Constitution:

> All persons connected in any way with this organization,
> and who may be entitled to full protection under it, shall be
> held as under obligation to labor in some way for the gen-
> eral good.

And in this society: "The punishment of crimes not
capital, shall be by hard labor on the public works."
It is a political and military axiom that in a time of revolution a new government forbids the carrying of arms if it
fears the people. Conversely, this government will allow
the bearing of arms if it believes it is ruling with the consent of the governed; such an arms-bearing people will
become a citizen's militia, ready to protect the new power.
John Brown was quite certain that his government would
be ruling *with* the consent of the majority. One of the
articles states:

> All persons known to be of good character, and of sound
> mind and suitable age, who are connected with this organ-
> ization, whether male or female, shall be encouraged to
> carry arms openly.

Note that women, as well as men, were encouraged to
bear arms. This in 1858. I am reminded of the lines in Walt
Whitman's poem, "Song Of The Broad Axe":

> Where women walk in public processions in
>   the streets the same as the men,
> Where they enter the public assembly and
>   take places the same as the men,
> Where the city of the faithfullest friends stands,
> Where the city of the cleanliness of the sexes stands,
> Where the city of the healthiest fathers stands,
> Where the city of the best-bodied mothers stands,
> There the great city stands.

The Provisional Constitution forbids "profane swearing, filthy conversation, indecent behavior," "indecent exposure," "intoxication," "unlawful intercourse of the sexes." Rape was punishable by death.

Schools and churches were to be established as soon as possible. The first day of the week was to be:

> A day of rest and appropriated to moral and religious instruction and improvement; relief to the suffering, instruction to the young and ignorant, and the encouragement of personal cleanliness; nor shall any person be required on that day to perform ordinary manual labor, unless in extremely urgent cases.

Because slaves were property from which a profit was to be derived, the slaveowners could not honor a marriage relationship between slaves. True, slaves were allowed to enter into a marriage, but they were marriages of convenience for the slaveowner. Families were broken up for reasons ranging from the sale of a slave to raise ready cash, to the dispersal of the entire slave family at the death of the slaveowner and the disposal of his goods. Slaves were sold on the auction block without recognition of the family structure as cows, horses and sheep were sold at a fair.

Nor was it uncommon for a female slave to have five or more children, each by a different father. Often some of these children were sired by the plantation owner—or by his son. However, the status of the father notwithstanding, the offspring of a slave mother was legally a slave. Sometimes these special slave children were given preferential treatment, even, occasionally, their freedom. Generally, however, they were treated as any other slave and subject to sale. This practice of selling off one's own child was fairly common. (Even Thomas Jefferson took slave women in concubinage. In the April, 1961 issue of *The Journal of Negro History*, Pearl M. Graham has a fascinating article about Thomas Jefferson and his relationship with Sally Hemings, his slave. Sally Hemings and her mother, Betty, were the property of John Wayles, whose daughter, Martha, married Thomas Jefferson. When John Wayles died, his property became Thomas Jefferson's since by right of law of that time, a married woman could hold no property; any property which came to her became in turn the absolute property of her husband. Pearl M. Graham writes about Betty Hemings and her daughter, Sally, "Sally was so much lighter in color than her mulatto mother as to justify the presumption that her father was white. Local gossip assigned her paternity, and that of her older siblings, to their master, John Wayles. If gossip spoke truth, Sally Hemings was half-sister to Mrs. Thomas Jefferson." Thomas Jefferson entered into a relationship with Sally Hemings when she was about 17 years old and over the years she bore him four or five children.)

John Brown expressed his feelings thus: "Any resistance, however bloody, is better than a system which makes every seventh woman a concubine."

Little wonder, then, that we find the following clause, designed to preserve the family unit. So great was his concern for broken slave families to be reunited that he wrote in a provision establishing a research bureau for this express purpose:

The marriage relationship shall be at all times respected; and families kept together as far as possible; and broken families encouraged to re-unite, and intelligence offices established for that purpose.

There were clauses pertaining to the destruction of property and to the treatment of prisoners. These were designed to provide a structure to restrain newly-freed slaves from wreaking vengeance and hate on their past masters:

The needless waste or destruction of any useful property or article, by fire, throwing open of fences, fields, buildings, or needless killing of animals, or injury of either, shall not be tolerated at any time or place, but shall be promptly and properly punished.

No person, after having surrendered himself a prisoner, shall afterward be put to death, or be subject to any corporal punishment, without first having had the benefit of a fair and impartial trial; nor shall any prisoner be treated with any kind of cruelty, disrespect, insult, or needless severity; but it shall be the duty of all persons, male or female, connected herewith, at all times and under all circumstances, to treat all such prisoners with every degree of respect and kindness the nature of the circumstances will admit of; and to insist on a like course of conduct from all others, or in the fear of Almighty God, to whose care and keeping we commit our course.

One instance of the bestiality of slavery will explain why John Brown wrote this protective clause into the Chatham Convention.

Each year, the Southern press carried thousands of advertisements serving notice of slaves who had fled. These advertisements contained descriptions to help identify and capture the fugitives: "Stamped NE on the breast and having both small toes cut off." "Has on a large neck iron on his left leg." "Branded on the left cheek, thus—'R,' and a piece is taken off her left ear on the same side; the same letter is branded on the inside of both legs." Yet John Brown demanded from slaves such as these that when freed they treat no prisoners with "cruelty, disrespect, insult or needless severity." On the contrary, it was demanded that such prisoners be treated "with every degree of respect and kindness."

There were two articles which complemented each other. One granted amnesty to the slaveholder, informing him that he could achieve remission of his sin by proper penance, which was the freeing of slaves.

The other article assured the non-slaveholder that his rights would be respected:

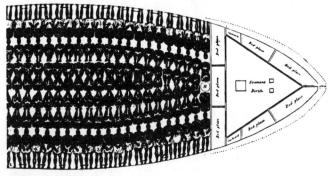

Plan of the lower deck of the slave ship Vigilante.

"The five rows in the center sat up during the whole voyage, extending over six weeks, or more according to the weather. During calm weather they were sometimes allowed on deck, but all the rest of the time they lay below with arms and legs manacled so that they could not move, in darkness, filth and nakedness. It was estimated that 30 percent died on the land journey, 12 percent of the survivors during the passage, 5 percent in harbour before the sale, and another third in 'seasoning.' So that of every hundred shipped only fifty lived to be labourers."

Traffic in "Black Gold." (From the New York Public Library, Schomburg Collection.)

Branding a slave.

GANG OF 25 SEA ISLAND
COTTON AND RICE NEGROES,

By LOUIS DE SAUSSURE.

On THURSDAY the 25th Sept., 1852, at 11 o'clock, A.M., will be sold at RYAN'S MART, in Chalmers Street, in the City of Charleston,

A prime gang of 25 Negroes, accustomed to the culture of Sea Island Cotton and Rice.

CONDITIONS.—One-half Cash, balance by Bond, bearing interest from day of sale, payable in one and two years, to be secured by a mortgage of the negroes and approved personal security. Purchasers to pay for papers.

(From the Collection of the Chicago Historical Society.)

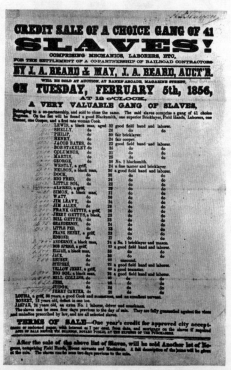

(From the Collection of the Chicago Historical Society.)

(From the Collection of the American Antiquarian Society.)

(From the New York Public Library, Schomburg Collection.)

A slave auction in the South. (Harper's Weekly, *1861.*)

"Belling" a slave to prevent escape.

Whipping and beating.

(From the New York Public Library, Schomburg Collection.)

Paddling and lashing.

The persons and property of all non-slaveholders who shall remain absolute neutral, shall be respected as far as the circumstances can allow of it; but they shall not be entitled to any active protection.

All persons who may come forward and shall voluntarily deliver up their slaves, and have their names registered on the Books of the organization, shall, so long as they continue at peace, be entitled to the fullest protection of person and property, though not connected with this organization, and shall be treated as friends, and not merely as persons neutral.

We see from this that John Brown was not concerned with killing slave masters. He *was* concerned that they renounce slavery.

There was an article designed to prevent a betrayal of the people by a secretly negotiated peace on the part of a few in authority:

Before any treaty of peace shall take full effect, it shall be signed by the President and Vice-President, the Commander-in-Chief, a majority of the House of Representatives, a majority of the Supreme Court, and majority of all general officers of the Army.

One more article remains to be discussed. It is Article 46, virtually the final article of the Provisional Constitution. A reading of the previously discussed articles of the Chatham Convention might lead one to believe that John Brown contemplated revolution. Although he planned to lead an armed band of guerrilla fighters into several states of the South, capture territory, set up a government within the enclave, hold the territory by force of arms, and also raid enemy territory, Article 46 explicitly denies revolutionary intent:

The foregoing Articles shall not be construed so as in any way to encourage the overthrow of any State Government of the United States; and look to no dissolution of the

Union, but simply to Amendment and Repeal and our flag shall be the same that our Fathers fought under in the Revolution.

John Brown's position, as expressed in Article 46, was a further and extended expression of his earlier position. I have discussed William Godwin and his *Enquiry Concerning Political Justice and Its Influence On Morals and Happiness*, as well as Henry Thoreau's *Civil Disobedience*. Both Godwin and Thoreau took the position that moral law was higher than man-made law and must take precedence over it. (As earlier stated, the thousands of citizens who helped fugitive slaves and so transgressed the Fugitive Slave Law were adherents to this position.) But with John Brown, a larger concept was involved. He believed that the continued existence of slavery threatened the Union and would ultimately destroy it. Slaveowners, therefore, were the conspirators and traitors; those who sought to destroy slavery were patriots defending the Union. To John Brown, the adherence to moral law was the highest expression of patriotism. Article 46 emanated from this principle.

Many historians, among them Oswald Garrison Villard in *John Brown: 1800-1859* and Hermann Von Holst in *John Brown*, have derided the Chatham Convention saying that John Brown's plans were so beyond the realm of realistic achievement, that they raise the question of aberration, if not downright insanity. I think they misread history. I suggest that such historians re-examine the Chatham Convention and John Brown's overall plan in the light of the success of guerrilla tactics in France, Yugoslavia, China, Italy, the Philippines and other areas during World War II.

But even more striking than the guerrilla experiences of World War II, are the similarities between John Brown's plans and those of Fidel Castro. After having trained in Mexico, Castro landed in Cuba with his army of 82 men in December, 1956. They were attacked by Batista's army and navy. Only 22 of the 82 survived, and ten of these were captured and imprisoned. Twelve managed to escape to the Sierra Mountains. One of the survivors reported that Castro said, "The days of the dictatorship are numbered." It was from the Sierra Mountains with his army of 11 men that Castro commenced his war against Batista's regular army of 40,000 men. As history has told us, the days of Batista *were* numbered. (I must emphasize here that I am *not* discussing the political aspects of Cuba and Castro. I am discussing the possibilities of realistic achievement of guerrilla warfare under given objective circumstances.)

At the Chatham Convention John Brown was elected Commander-in-Chief; John Henri Kagi, his second-in-command, was elected Secretary of War; Richard Realf, a journalist and poet whom we shall soon encounter in another context, was appointed Secretary of State. (John Henri Kagi was at that time 23 years old. He was born in a little town in Ohio where his father was a blacksmith. At the age of 19 he was teaching school in Virginia; here he learned about slavery at first hand. However, he was so outspoken, that he had to leave rather hastily. He returned to Ohio; there he taught school, studied law, earned a reputation as a superb debater, and worked as a newspaper reporter, meanwhile teaching himself stenography. Kagi was next heard from in Nebraska, where he was admitted to the bar at the age of 21. He travelled to Kansas to help in the fight there. He joined a militia, served for a year, was captured and imprisoned for four months. During all this time in Kansas he was a working journalist, writing for *The New York Evening Post, The New York Tribune, The Chicago Tribune, The Cleveland Leader,* and the *National Era* in Washington. He wrote with great vigor and lucidity and was a thorn to the pro-slavers who finally arrested him by a ruse. In an excellent sketch of Kagi to be found in Richard J. Hinton's *John Brown and His Men*, Hinton writes, "The purpose of his arrest was evidently to stop his pen. But it only increased its usefulness, for prison letters bitterly incisive in their exposure of brutal cruelty, were of great value in the creation of Northern public opinion." Kagi met John Brown in Topeka, Kansas, during October, 1857, and for the next two years, until October, 1859, when Kagi was killed during the raid on Harpers Ferry, their relationship was strong and close. Hinton also writes, "Mentally he was the ablest of those who followed John Brown to Harper's Ferry. In the best sense, too, he was the most scholarly and cultured.")

John Brown's activity was unceasing from the day he knocked at Frederick Douglass's door late in January, 1858, to mid-May of that same year. At Douglass's home he wrote the Provisional Constitution; then to Peterboro, New York, and Boston to rally support and money; then to Philadelphia to confer with Negro leaders in the Underground Railroad; then back to Gerrit Smith in Peterboro to consolidate his support; then back to Rochester and Frederick Douglass; on to St. Catherine's to confer with Harriet Tubman and to lay out plans for the Chatham Convention; back to Iowa where his men were working and training, to collect and bring them to Chatham; and, finally, the Chatham Convention.

All was in readiness. The intention had been to start for the Harpers Ferry area from Chatham immediately after the Convention. Richard Realf wrote to one of John Brown's men who could not get to the Convention:

> Here we intend to remain till we have perfected our plans, which will be in about ten days or two weeks, after which we start for *China*. The signals and mode of writing are (the old man informs me) all arranged. Remember me to all who know our business, but to all others be as dumb as death.

The date of the attack was quite probably set for July 4,

1858. John Brown well understood the nature of evocative symbols; the idea of striking on Independence Day would certainly have appealed to him.

Then came the blow which shattered these years of planning.

John Brown had hired a drill master and assistant, Hugh Forbes by name, who proved to be a blackmailer. First, he demanded salaries which had not been promised to him. John Brown could ill afford such sums from his painfully gathered contributions. Though galled by the situation, he tried to make peace with Forbes by giving him additional money. But Forbes was not to be quieted. After making exorbitant demands on John Brown's New England supporters, he collected whatever he could from them, threatening to reveal the plan to pro-slavery forces.

John Brown, in Canada, working on the Convention, did not know that events had come to such a head with Forbes until he received a letter from his New England supporters, the Secret Six, dated May 10, the last day of the Convention. John Brown wrote back:

> I have only time to say at this moment that as it is an invariable rule with me to be governed by circumstances, or, in other words, not to do anything while I do not know what to do, none of our friends need have any fear in relation to hasty or rash steps being taken by us. As knowledge is said to be power, we propose to become possessed of more knowledge. None of us here or with you should be hasty, or decide the course to be taken, while under excitement.

There was considerable dissension among the Secret Six as to how to proceed. John Brown, after careful evaluation of the situation, decided that the best course was to move at once before anyone would have time to act on Forbes's information. In this he was seconded by Higginson, who wrote:

I regard any postponement as simply abandoning the project; for if we give it up now, at the command or threat of Hugh Forbes, it will be the same next year. When the thing is well started, who cares what he says?

John Brown and Higginson were overruled. It was decided that John Brown should return to Kansas. This would throw everyone off the track and make Forbes's conduct seem foolish and unfounded.

John Brown had exhausted the relatively small funds he had received. He was virtually penniless and stranded in Chatham. It was a shattering blow, but he agreed to go to Kansas.

Everything had seemed ready and in perfect focus; now all was disjointed by Forbes's threatened betrayal. John Brown dispersed his men into small groups, instructing them to take whatever jobs they could find to support themselves until such time as he could gather them together again. This dispersal cost him five of the men he had brought to the Chatham Convention. During the intervening time, various personal events entered into their lives, and when John Brown called, they did not respond.

* * * * * *

John Brown arrived in Kansas in June, 1858, his third trip into the Territory.

I have already described the first interview John Brown had with William A. Phillips during July, 1856, and the night journey they took to Topeka. Late in 1858, Phillips had the last of his interviews with John Brown (as you recall, these were published in 1879):

He had changed a little. There was in the expression of his face something even more dignified than usual; his eye was brighter, and the absorbing and consuming thoughts that were within him seemed to be growing out all over him.

He sketched the history of American slavery from its beginnings in the colonies, and referred to the States that were able to shake it off. He said the founders of the republic were all opposed to slavery, and that the whole spirit and genius of the American constitution antagonized it, and contemplated its early overthrow. He said this remained the dominant sentiment for the first quarter of a century of the republic. Afterwards slavery became more profitable, and as it did, the desire grew to extend and increase it. The slave-trade being ended, it was profitable to breed negroes for sale. Gradually the pecuniary interests that rested on slavery seized the power of the government.

The politicans of the South became slavery propagandists, and the politicians of the North trimmers. When the religious and moral sentiment of the country indicated a desire to check this alarming growth, a threat of secession was uttered, and appeals were made not to risk the perpetuation of this glorious republic by fanatical anti-slaveryism. Then began an era of political compromises, and men full of professions of love of country were willing, for peace, to sacrifice everything for which the republic was founded.

"And now," he went on, "we have reached a point where nothing but war can settle the question. They never intend to relinquish the machinery of this government into the hands of the opponents of slavery. It has taken them more than half a century to get it, and they know its significance too well to give it up. If the Republican party elects its president next year, there will be war. The moment they are unable to control they will go out, and as a rival nation along-side they will get the countenance and aid of the European nations, until American republicanism and freedom are overthrown."

The whole powers of his mind (and they were great) had been given to one subject. He told me that a war was at that very moment contemplated in the cabinet of President Buchanan; that for years the army had been carefully arranged, as far as it could be, on a basis of Southern power; that arms and the best of the troops were being concentrated, so as to be under control of its interests if there was danger of having to surrender the government; that the secretary of the navy was then sending our vessels away on long cruises, so that they would not be available, and that the treasury would be beggared before it got into Northern hands.

All this has a strangely prophetic look to me now; then it simply appeared incredible, or the dream and vagary of a man who had allowed one idea to carry him away. I told him he surely was mistaken, and had confounded every day occurrences with treacherous designs.

"No," he said,—and I remember this part distinctly—, "no, the war is not over. It is a treacherous lull before the storm. We are on the eve of one of the greatest wars in history, and I fear slavery will triumph, and there will be an end of all aspirations for human freedom. For my part, I drew my sword in Kansas when they attacked us, and I will never sheathe it until this war is over. Our best people do not understand the danger. They are besotted. They have compromised so long that they think principles of right and wrong have no more any power on this earth."

I told him that I feared he would lead the young men with him into some desperate enterprise, where they would be imprisoned and disgraced.

He rose. "Well," he said, "I thought I could get you to understand this. I do not wonder at it. The world is very pleasant to you; but when your household gods are broken, as mine have been, you will see all this more clearly."

I rose, somewhat offended, and walked to the door.

He followed me, and laid his hand on my shoulder, and when I turned to him he took both my hands in his. I could see that tears stood on his hard, bronzed cheeks. "No," he said, "we must not part thus. I wanted to see you and tell you how it appeared to me. With the help of God, I will do what I believe to be best." He held my hands firmly in his stern, hard hands, leaned forward and kissed me on the cheek, and I never saw him again.

Phillips, from the vantage point of 1879, comments that

[86]

the warning of John Brown "has a strangely prophetic look to me now; then it seemed incredible."

How right John Brown was; his grasp of both the over-all national scene and specific detail was extraordinary. The Republican Party *did* elect Lincoln; the South immediately set the wheels in motion to secede. Secretary of War John Floyd, a former governor of Virginia, foreseeing the eventuality of secession and civil war, had been shipping the most modern arms to the South, sending inferior arms to the North. (John Floyd joined the Confederate forces and became a brigadier-general.)

As for John Brown's statement about "sending our vessels away on long cruises, so that they would not be available," the history of the naval blockade reveals the acuteness of his perception. In 1861, when Lincoln declared a blockade on the Southern coastline, forbidding all ships on pain of capture and confiscation to attempt to enter Southern ports, the United States Navy had only *three* ships available for the blockade. This coastline was 3,500 miles long—less than one ship for every thousand miles.

The United States Navy did, in fact, possess about 50 vessels which could have been engaged in the blockade; but they were scattered all over the globe—South and Central America, China and other remote places. It took a full six months to bring these vessels back and employ them in the blockade. Eventually, the Federal Government was able to concentrate a force of 600 ships against Southern ports; but for the first year of the war, the blockade, though an instrument of the Federal Government, was as good as nonexistent.

Ironically, during that first year of war, although the blockade was almost totally inoperative, the Confederate Government determined not to ship cotton to England and France. By means of its self-imposed embargo, the South thought it could force England and France to recognize the Confederacy at once, since both those countries were economically dependent upon cotton. However, the cotton embargo was a gross Confederate miscalculation. While it did throw millions of workers into a state of unemployment in Europe, and subjected the British and French governments to diplomatic pressure, the embargo also inflicted such severe injury on the economy of the Confederacy that it never recovered.

At the outbreak of the Civil War, the South had on hand four million bales of cotton. At $500 a bale, the cotton was worth two billion dollars. Had only a small fraction of this crop been sold, it could have been the central means of financing the war.

After the war, when President Jefferson Davis was a prisoner, he bemoaned the fact that the Confederacy had not shipped cotton during the early stages of the war. Had they, "acted favorably on the proposition of depositing cotton in Europe and holding it there for two years as a basis for their currency, their circulating medium might have maintained itself at par to the closing day of the struggle, and that in itself would have assured the victory."

Perhaps Jefferson Davis was too sanguine about the "assured victory," but he was correct about the great error made in not shipping cotton to England and France. By the time the Confederate Government recognized its basic blunder and decided to ship cotton, it was too late. The blockade had begun to function, and with each passing month became increasingly effective. Later, when Northern troops marched into the South, the South adopted the policy of burning warehouses full of cotton to prevent their falling into the hands of the North.

Union men were convinced that the vessels of our navy *were* deliberately scattered throughout the world to ensure the failure of a blockade in a war which the South thought would be of less than a year's duration—thus echoing John Brown's thought which he enunciated to Phillips in late 1858 just prior to his leaving Kansas for the last time.

[88]

* * * * * *

John Brown was not greatly needed during this stay in Kansas. True, his name inspired terror and his mere presence acted as a deterrent. But the North, due to the efforts of various emigrant aid societies, had already won the battle of settlers. Further, responsible citizens of both sides, weary of years of marauding bands, were earnestly trying to achieve stability.

By December, 1858, John Brown was more than ready for Harpers Ferry, but before leaving the West he was involved in one last turbulent episode. He was told of five slaves living in Missouri, close to the border, who were to be sold at auction. He organized some of his men into a raiding party and, on the night of December 20, 1858, they forcibly liberated not only these five, but six others in addition. John Brown crossed back from Missouri into Kansas Territory with his 11 rescued slaves. These 11 slaves were soon to be augmented by a twelfth, a boy born on the way and christened John Brown.

Then began a long slow journey northward through Kansas, Nebraska and Iowa in the dead of winter. They traveled by ox team, later by horse and wagon. To protect his charges, John Brown had two, often only one man, to accompany him on this journey. The prairie snow storms were relentless. John Brown's fingers, nose, and ears were frozen. Near Topeka, a farmer, who later related the incident, gave John Brown a sorely needed article of clothing:

I came down that night with him to cross the river, and on the way he told me he had some colored people with him, who were in need, and asked me if I could do anything to help them. They had no shoes, and but little to eat. I went out among the houses and into several stores and got a number of pairs of shoes and some little money for the good cause. As we were going down to the river, I noticed Brown shivering, and that his legs trembled a good deal. I suspected something, and as I sat beside him on my horse I

[89]

reached down and felt of his pantaloons, and found they were of cotton, thin and suited to summer, not to the cold weather we had then. I asked him: "Mr. Brown, have you no drawers?" He said he had not. "Well," I said, "there is no time to go to the store now; but I have on a pair that were new today, and if you will take them you can have them and welcome." After a few words he agreed to it. We got down beside the wagons; I took the drawers off, and he put them on.

They plodded on northward across the frozen, storm-beaten plains towards Canada, outwitting a dozen pursuing parties intent on capturing the runaway slaves—and claiming, as well, the reward of $250 offered by the United States Government for the capture of John Brown.

By March 9, 1859, almost 80 days after his foray into Missouri, he and his band of fugitives had traversed a distance of 600 miles and had reached a little town in the northeastern part of Iowa. Through the aid of some railroad people, the fugitives were secretly led into a box car, which was later hooked onto a train going to Chicago; from there, by another box car to Detroit. At Detroit they were put on the ferry which brought them to Windsor, Canada, and freedom.

John Brown's raids into Missouri threw the slaveowners along the border into a state of fear. More than anything else the slaveholders dreaded the flight of slaves into freedom. Such flight was contagious, disaffecting slaves for miles about; this financial bleeding had endless repercussions. In fact, slaveowners for a distance of twenty and more miles from the area of John Brown's incursion moved their slaves further south, or kept them under heavy guard.

Many a marshal and posse tried to capture John Brown. Most he outwitted; the others lost their nerve at the critical moment because it was well known that he would not be taken alive. He was experienced at dodging capture. Two years earlier, during April, 1857, upon learning that a United States deputy marshal was out for him because of his Kansas activities, he wrote:

> One of U.S. Hounds is on my track; And I have kept myself hid for a few days to let my track get cold. I have no idea of being taken; and intend (if "God will") to go back with irons *in* rather than *upon* my hands.

The place where John Brown kept himself "hid for a few days" was Judge Thomas Russell's home in Boston. Judge Russell recalled that, "He used to take out his two revolvers and repeater every night before going to bed, to make sure of their loads, saying, 'Here are eighteen lives.'" And to Mrs. Russell, John Brown once said, "If you hear a noise at night, put the baby under the pillow. I would hate to spoil these carpets, too, but you know I cannot be taken alive."

Part III

"It is not desirable to cultivate a respect for the law, so much as for the right. If the law is of such a nature that it requires you to be an agent of injustice to another, then, I say, break the law. Let your life be a counterfriction to stop the machine."

Henry David Thoreau:
Civil Disobedience.

During July, 1859, John Brown rented the Kennedy farmhouse, five miles from Harpers Ferry. He arranged for some of the women of his family to come from North Elba; posing as a farmer, he began to gather his men and his arms. The nucleus of his band were the men who had fought with him in Kansas, plus the new recruits who had drilled and trained during 1857 and 1858. In addition, he had counted on further recruits to come from Kansas and the East, and also former slaves who had escaped into Canada.

One of the men John Brown recruited in Kansas Territory during the summer of 1858 was Richard J. Hinton, a journalist. (Hinton was en route to the Kennedy farmhouse in October, 1859, but turned back when he learned that the raid had already taken place.) Hinton wrote a detailed account of how he was recruited. This account was first published early in 1860 in James Redpath's *The Public Life Of Captain John Brown*, only a few months after John Brown was hanged. Subsequently, Hinton's recollections appeared in his own book, *John Brown And His Men*, published in 1894. Hinton writes:

Kagi unfolded the whole of their plans. The mountains of Virginia were named as the place of refuge, and as a country admirably adapted in which to carry on a guerilla warfare. In the course of the conversation, Harper's Ferry was mentioned as a point to be seized, but not held,—on account of the Arsenal. The white members of the company were to act as officers of different guerrilla bands, which, under the general command of John Brown, were to be composed of Canadian refugees, and the Virginia slaves who would join them. They anticipated, after the first blow had been struck, that, by the aid of the free and Canadian negroes, they could inspire confidence in the slaves, and induce them to rally. No intention was expressed of gathering a large body of slaves, and removing them to Canada. On the contrary, Kagi clearly stated, in answer to my inquiries, that the design was to make the fight in the mountains of Virginia, extending it to North Carolina and Tennessee, and also to the swamps of South Carolina if possible. *Their purpose was not the extradition of one or a thousand slaves, but their liberation in the States wherein they were born, and were now held in bondage.*

Kagi spoke of having marked out a chain of counties extending continuously through South Carolina, Georgia, Alabama and Mississippi. The counties he named were those which contained the largest proportion of slaves, and would, therefore, be the best in which to strike. The blow struck at Harper's Ferry was to be in the Spring, when the planters were busy, and the slaves most needed. The arms in the Arsenal were to be taken to the mountains, with such slaves as joined. The telegraph wires were to be cut, and the railroad tracks torn up in all directions. As fast as possible other bands besides the original ones were to be formed, and a continuous chain of posts established in the mountains. They expected to be speedily and constantly reinforced; first, by the arrival of those men, who, in Canada, were anxiously looking and praying for the time of deliverance, and then by the slaves themselves. Kagi said one of the reasons that induced him to go into the enterprise was a full conviction that at no very distant day forcible efforts for freedom would break out among the slaves. Believing that such a blow would soon be struck, he wanted *to organize it so as to make it more effectual,* and also, by directing and controlling the negroes, to prevent some of the atrocities that would necessarily arise from the sudden upheaval of such a mass as the Southern slaves.

Hinton describes the conversation he had with Kagi regarding Harpers Ferry:

Kagi, when telling me of the plan, had emphasized the intention of getting out of the place before the frightened people could get organized for an attack in force.

Hinton also writes that John Cook, who had been sent several months earlier by John Brown to spy out the land, and had drawn maps of both Harpers Ferry and the surrounding area, had "made many visits to examine and report on the Government buildings, their contents, weak or strong points, habits of their watchman, and other matters of value."

This plan of John Brown's was explicitly reconfirmed under entirely different circumstances. On December 14, 1859, 12 days after John Brown was hanged, the Congress of the United States appointed a committee to "Inquire Into The Facts Attending The Late Invasion And Seizure Of The United States Armory At Harper's Ferry, Virginia." Senator James M. Mason of Virginia, who in 1850 introduced the Fugitive Slave Law on the floor of the Senate, was Chairman of this Congressional Committee; Senator Jefferson Davis of Mississippi, future President of the Confederacy, was also a member. One of the men who appeared before the Committee was Richard Realf, the poet and journalist, who had been appointed Secretary of State at the Chatham Convention. He was to have been a member of the raiding party, but defected. The Committee examined him on January 21, 1860, approximately a month and a half after John Brown was hanged. A member of the Committee asked Richard Realf for details of the plan which John Brown had laid before the delegates to the Chatham Convention. Here follows that section of the testimony:

Question: Do you recollect Brown's speech, which "developed the plan"?

Answer: John Brown stated that for twenty or thirty years the idea had possessed him like a passion of giving liberty to the slaves. He stated that he had read all the books upon insurrectionary warfare which he could lay his hands upon—the successful opposition of the Spanish chieftains during the period when Spain was a Roman province; how with ten thousand men divided and subdivided into small companies, acting simultaneously, yet separately, they withstood the whole consolidated power of the Roman empire through a number of years. He said he had posted himself in relation to the wars of Toussaint L'Ouverture; he had become thoroughly acquainted with the war in Haiti; and from all these things he had drawn the conclusion that upon the first intimation the slaves would immediately rise all over the Southern States. He supposed that they would come into the mountains to join him, and that by flocking to his standard they would enable him (by making the line of mountains which cuts diagonally through Maryland and Virginia down through the Southern States into Tennessee and Alabama, the base of his operations) to act upon the plantations on the plains lying on each side of that range of mountains, and that we should be able to establish ourselves in the fastnesses, and then organize the freed blacks under this provisional constitution. They were to be taught the useful and mechanical arts, and to be

[95]

instructed in all the business of life. Schools were also to be established.

Question: Did he develop in that plan where he expected to get aid or assistance; who were to be his soldiers?

Answer: The negroes were to constitute the soldiers. John Brown expected that all the free negroes in the Northern States would immediately flock to his standard. He expected that all the slaves in the Southern States would do the same. He believed, too, that as many of the free negroes in Canada as could accompany him, would do so.

Question: Was anything said after he got into the slave States, of any division of sentiment between the slaveholders and non-slaveholders?

Answer: The slaveholders were to be taken as hostages, if they refused to let their slaves go. It is a mistake to suppose that they were to be killed. They were to be held as hostages for the safe treatment of any prisoners of John Brown's who might fall into the hands of hostile parties.

Question: As to the non-slaveholders; was there anything said about them?

Answer: All the non-slaveholders were to be protected. Those who would not join the organization of John Brown, but who would not oppose it, were to be protected; but those who did oppose it, were to be treated as the slaveholders themselves.

This, then, was John Brown's plan. Harpers Ferry was to be the first step of a large comprehensive design. He planned to hold Harpers Ferry for a short time, during which period he would seize arms and ammunition from the captured Federal Government Armory and Arsenal. Then, gathering up whatever slaves came to his banner, he would retreat into the fastnesses of the Alleghenies.

Once in the Alleghenies, operating as a guerrilla force, moving ever deeper into the South as his strength grew, John Brown planned to swoop down on the lowlands, attack, gather up slaves, and retreat back into the mountains. He would augment his forces from the bolder and stronger slaves; the less able would be sent via the mountain route northward to freedom. Such attacks would make it unsafe to possess slaves; they would expose the system's inherent weakness, for such stampedes could not but "destroy the money value of slave property."

A study of the map of this area shows the great possibility of success once John Brown got out of Harpers Ferry. I repeat—*once John Brown got out of Harpers Ferry*. A hard climb of an hour or two would have taken John Brown and his men to safety in the foothills of the Alleghenies. Another few hours and they would have been in the mountain wilderness where caves, deep ravines and natural fortresses would allow ten men to hold off a hundred.

The Alleghenies were The Great Black Way, the main route which thousands of slaves took to freedom. These mountains begin in Alabama, sprawl in a northeasterly direction clear up to the free state of Pennsylvania, and continue into the northern sections of New York State. Virginia was a central and strategic spot, located at the mid-point of this majestic and wild chain. Thus, John Brown could push down into the South, yet keep open a line of communication into the North by means of Pennsylvania.

John Brown had said, "God had established the Allegheny Mountains from the foundation of the world that they may one day be a refuge for fugitive slaves." And also, "A few men in the right, and knowing they are, can overturn a king. Twenty men in the Alleghenies could break slavery to pieces in two years." Speaking of Nat Turner's revolt in 1831 which paralyzed Virginia, he had said, "Nat Turner, with fifty men, held Virginia for five weeks. The same number, well organized and armed, can shake the system out of the State." He was going to put this amalgam into operation.

To understand the possibilities of success for John

Brown once he reached the mountains, it is necessary to review the state of communications and weaponry of that period. In those days there were no motor transport and aviation; radio, telephone and radar; tanks, rockets, machine guns and highly mobile cannon. Indeed, during the Civil War, cavalry was the most mobile force for attack and transport, and was used as the "eyes" by both armies for scouting and spying. However, in the trackless and virtually impenetrable wilderness of the Alleghenies, even cavalry would have had severely limited uses. Foot soldiers with rifles were the only force that could have been mustered against John Brown; and against these John Brown could have maintained the initiative.

No guerrilla force can exist for long on the land without, first, the acquiescence, and then the support, of the native population. A hostile people will betray the presence of such a force to the authorities, who, with their superior numbers and arms, can destroy the guerrillas. Thus, since John Brown planned to press into the South and operate in the Alleghenies, it is necessary to examine the texture of this native population.

The area in which John Brown intended to operate was a vast expanse of land, approximately 500 miles deep and 200 miles wide, bounded by the Blue Ridge Mountains on one side and the Cumberland and other ranges on the other. On this mighty jut of land protruding into the heart of the South, small farmers scrabbled out a living with their own hands. In derogation, they were called hillbillies, crackers and poor whites, as today they are called hillbillies, crackers and poor whites.

Working on impoverished soil, these farmers had nothing in common with the wealthy cotton, tobacco and sugar planters whose plantations stretched across the coastal plains, the Tidewater and the Piedmont areas. For more than 50 years, the plantation owners had restricted the political power of the mountain farmers in favor of their own economic interests.

[98]

In addition to class division, there were also divisions of ethnic and religious backgrounds. The up-country people were, in the main, Scotch-Irish in descent, and Baptist, Methodist and Presbyterian by faith, as opposed to the Anglican plantation owners of the Tidewater and Piedmont regions.

The conduct of this poverty-stricken mountain class during the Civil War is most interesting. For a hundred years, the myth has been propagated that the entire South stood up as one man, loyally and gallantly, to serve under the Confederate flag. Nothing could be further from the truth. This myth still flourishes despite the appearance during the 1920s and 1930s of three books: *Conscription And Conflict In The Confederacy* by Albert B. Moore, *Desertion During The Civil War* by Ella Lonn, and *Disloyalty In The Confederacy* by Georgia Lee Tatum.

The fact is that two distinct groupings existed in the South—at war with each other within the Confederacy, just as fiercely as the Confederacy was at war with the Union.

The people living on the vast stretch of mountainous land which I have described, were opposed to secession and voted against it; when secession became a fact, they remained loyal to the Union. Western Virginia broke away from Virginia, formed the state of West Virginia, and affirmed its allegiance to the Union. The eastern section of Tennessee planned to form its own state and join the Union. Though the attempt failed, the pro-Union loyalty of this section remained a thorn to the Confederates. (This explains, in part, why the Republican Party selected Andrew Johnson of East Tennessee as its candidate for the Vice-President in 1864. The assassination of Lincoln put Johnson of East Tennessee into the White House.)

Nearly every county in southwestern Virginia, the western sections of North and South Carolina, eastern Tennessee, the northern sections of Georgia and Alabama, had secret societies whose principal object was to agitate for

[99]

peace and a return to the Union. They discouraged enlistment in the Confederate Army and encouraged desertion; they fought Confederate conscription laws and encouraged enlistment in the Union Army. The South had a provision in its conscription laws as did the North, which allowed a drafted man to be exempted if he could afford to purchase a substitute. In addition to this form of exemption, the South enacted what soon became known as the "twenty nigger law," a law which exempted from military service one person, either owner or overseer, for every 20 slaves. For example, an owner of 60 slaves could claim exemption for himself and two overseers. Later, the number of slaves required for each exemption was reduced from 20 to 15. Senator James Phelan of Mississippi wrote President Davis in December, 1862, "It seems as if nine-tenths of the youngsters of the land whose relatives are conspicuous in society, wealthy or influential, obtain some safe perch where they can doze with their heads under their wings." He warned Davis that no law had ever met "with more universal odium than the exemption of slave-owners. Its influence upon the poor is most calamitous, and has awakened a spirit and elicited a discussion of which we may safely predict the most unfortunate results."

Senator Phelan was quite right. The mountain people turned their back on this rich man's war. Many a conscription agent was shot dead while trying to carry out his orders. The mountain people had no desire to die for the wealthy aristocrats who were living in sumptuous elegance on the rich lands below.

The Southern leadership was aware of the risk it was taking when it passed the "twenty nigger law," but it was caught in a dilemma from which it couldn't extricate itself. The law establishing a one-out-of-twenty ratio of exemption was needed to supply the manpower to supervise production on plantation and farm; moreover, it was also needed as a home guard to keep disaffection in check. The turbulence among slaves increased with the continuation of the war, and a stronger home guard was needed. Entrapped in a vise of their own contradictions, the South changed the ratio of exemption from 20 to 15—and further exacerbated the already inflamed condition of the mountain people. This pinning down of able-bodied male population to guard the rear had an adverse effect at the front, where the manpower shortage became more critical with each passing month.

As for desertions, what began as a trickle, ended as a flood. In the very first year of the war men deserted in groups of two, three and four. By September, 1862, General Lee, in an attempt to stop the increasing desertions, wrote to Jefferson Davis, "Some immediate legislation is required and the most summary punishment should be authorized. It ought to be construed into desertion in the face of the enemy, and thus brought under the Rules and Articles of War."

By 1863, to take but one example from many, it was estimated that one-half of the soldiers from the northeastern counties of Georgia were hiding in the mountains. The Confederate War Office stated to its Secretary of State, Seddon, "The condition of things in the mountain districts of North Carolina, South Carolina, Georgia and Alabama menaces the existence of the Confederacy as fatally as either of the armies of the United States."

Tens of thousands of these deserters lived in caves, swamps and forests. Perhaps a good percentage of them deserted because of the accelerating disintegration of the Confederate Army—increasing shortages of food, clothing, shoes, weapons. This was not true of other tens of thousands of deserters who crossed the line and volunteered for the Union Army; they took the Union oath of allegiance for ideological reasons—some were motivated by moral conviction, others by class identity.

By 1864, General Grant stated that the Confederate Army was losing a regiment a day due to desertion. During March, 1865, Lee lost an entire brigade and wrote to his War Department, complaining bitterly about this mass defection.

Two situations, which occurred in 1864, are worth examining side by side. When Sherman captured Atlanta, and then carried out his famous march to the sea—from Atlanta to Savannah—his army actually increased in numbers during the course of the march. This increase was brought about because thousands of up-country Southerners, such as those I have been describing, volunteered along the way. In contrast, President Davis of the Confederacy, in a speech at Macon, Georgia, that same year, estimated that about two-thirds of Hood's army had deserted. Lee's dispatches of that period frequently refer to desertion:

> November 18, 1864: Desertion is increasing in the army notwithstanding all my efforts to stop it.

> January 27, 1865: I call to your attention to the alarming frequency of desertion from this army.

> February 25, 1865: Hundreds of men are deserting nightly and I cannot keep the army together unless examples are made of such cases.

His dispatch of February 28, 1865, reports 1,094 desertions in 10 days; On March 27, 1865, he reports 1,061 desertions in 10 days. His despair is evident when he writes, "I do not know what can be done to put a stop to it."

When John Brown envisaged his plan to destroy slavery, it was to these dissenting mountain people that he looked for support. There can be small doubt that several articles of the Provisional Constitution of the Chatham Convention of 1858 had been written specifically with them in mind, and with a view to winning them over quickly. John Brown expected they would scout for him, conceal the presence of his forces, tend his wounded, give him food when necessary; and further, that some of them would join his army.

This vast plan of John Brown's needed a dramatic opening trumpet to announce to black and white that war was inevitable. Harpers Ferry would serve this function.

*   *   *   *   *   *

During the summer and fall of 1859, John Brown was at the Kennedy farmhouse collecting both his arms and his men. The arms, marked as "agricultural implements," were shipped by freight to Chambersburg, Pennsylvania; from there, they went to the farmhouse by horse and wagon. These trips were made at night to avoid the frequent road patrols. In all the slave states, road patrols were on the constant alert for fugitive slaves, or for any suspicious circumstances which might require investigation.

At the farmhouse, extreme vigilance was exercised lest the growing band of men be discovered. John Brown had to adhere to his role of a farmer with sons and womenfolk. One of the women sat on the porch sewing, knitting or reading, keeping a constant lookout. When she gave warning of an approaching neighbor, all the extra men had to take every vestige of their belongings—sometimes the very food they were eating—and flee up to the attic, staying there without sound or movement until they received a signal from below that all was clear.

The farmhouse was small and with each new arrival it became more crowded. None of "the invisibles," as the men came to be called, were allowed out during the day lest they be spotted and the house investigated. The "invisibles" passed the interminable days of waiting by playing checkers and cards, fashioning belts and holsters for themselves, cleaning and oiling rifles and pistols in preparation for the raid, and by debating all manner of sub-

[103]

jects. One of the men, undaunted, diligently practiced shorthand.

Occasionally there was a summer thunderstorm. Then these young men, accustomed to vigorous outdoor life, broke the bonds of their confining quarters. They would dash out into the open, jumping and shouting, knowing they were safe, for the howling summer storm covered their noise.

As is true of most armies, all but one of these men were young, ranging in age from 20 to 32. The three youngest were John Brown's son, Oliver, Barclay Coppoc and William Leeman, all aged 20. Shortly before the attack on Harpers Ferry, William Leeman writes to his mother:

I am now in a Southern *slave State,* and before I leave it, it will be a free State, and so *will every other one in the South.* Yes, Mother, I am warring with slavery, the greatest curse that ever infested America. We are determined to strike for freedom, incite the slaves to rebellion, and establish a free government. With the help of God we will carry it through. Now you will see, Mother, the reason why I have stayed away from you so long—why I have never helped you when I knew you was in want, and why I have not explained to you before. I dared not divulge it. I am in a good cause and I am not afraid. I know my mother will not object. You have a generous heart. I know you will sacrifice something for your fellow beings in bondage.

And Jeremiah Anderson, aged 27, writes to his brother:

Our mining company will consist of between twenty-five and thirty well equipped with tools. Millions of fellow beings require it of us; their cries for help go out to the universe daily and hourly. Whose duty it is to help them? Is it yours, is it mine? It is every man's; but how few there are to help. There are a few who dare to answer this call, and dare to answer it in a manner that will make this land of Liberty and Equality shake to the center. If my life is sacrificed, it can't be lost in a better cause. Our motto is, "We go to win at all hazards." But that is the last of our thoughts. The old man had had this operation in view for twenty years. It is not a large place, but a precious one to Uncle Sam, as he has a great many tools there. I expect (when I start again traveling) to start at that place, and go through the State of Virginia and on South, just as circumstances requiring mining, and prospecting, and carrying the *ore* along with us.

Oliver Brown married Martha Brewster, a neighbor in North Elba, during April, 1858, when he was 19 and she 16. Seventeen months after their marriage, they were both at the Kennedy farmhouse; he, in preparation for the attack on Harpers Ferry, she to carry out the fiction that an ordinary farmer's family was living at the farmhouse. Martha arrived at the Kennedy farm shortly after becoming pregnant. A few weeks before the attack on Harpers Ferry, John Brown sent the women of his family home so that they would be out of danger. Oliver writes to his 17-year-old pregnant wife, now safely back in North Elba:

You can hardly think how I want to see you, or how lonesome it was the day I left you. Nothing else could strengthen me to do the right so much as the thought of you. It is when I look at your picture that I am wholly ashamed of my every meanness, weakness and folly. I would not part with that picture for anything on earth—but the original. I have made a morocco case for it and carry it close around my body. I am more and more determined every day to live a more unselfish life.

Now, Martha, you can hardly conceive my great anxiety about you in your present situation, and you will certainly allow me to suggest some ideas to you for your own good. Let me ask you to try to keep up good, cheerful spirits. Take plenty of sleep and rest, plenty of outdoor exercise. Bathe often. And, finally, do read good books, such as Parker's "Sermons" and Combe's "Constitution of Man." These books will do much to keep you from being lonesome.

Finally, Martha, do try to enjoy yourself. Make the best of everything. Remember your affectionate husband.

Oliver was killed at Harpers Ferry, and this letter of his, dated October 9, 1859, did not reach Martha until after she had received news of his death. Martha, too, was soon to die. Her child, Olive, was born during February, 1860, and died two days later. Martha lingered one month after the child, and died on March 2. Shortly before she died, she mourned, "Other women give money, but I have given all; my beloved and my life."

Watson Brown, aged 24, was also to die at Harpers Ferry. Shortly before he left for the Kennedy farmhouse, his wife, Isabella, affectionately called Bell, had given birth to a boy. Watson writes to Bell:

You can guess how I long to see you only by knowing how you wish to see me. I think of you all day, and dream of you at night. I would gladly come home and stay with you always but for the cause which brought me here—a desire to do something for others, and not live wholly for my own happiness.

And Bell replies: "Now, Watson, keep up good courage and do not worry about me and come back as soon as possible. I think of you all night in my dreams."

And Watson again writes:

I sometimes feel as though I could not make the sacrifice, but what would I want others to do, were I in their place? Oh, Bell, I do want to see you and the little fellow very much, but I must wait. There was a slave near here whose wife was sold off South the other day, and he was found in Thomas Kennedy's orchard, dead, the next morning. I cannot come home as long as such things are done here. There was another murder committed near our place the other day, making in all five murders and one suicide within five miles of our place since we have lived here.

Thomas Wentworth Higginson

Theodore Parker

Franklin Benjamin Sanborn

George Luther Stearns

Samuel Gridley Howe

Gerrit Smith

The Secret Six

Watson Brown, son of John Brown. He was killed at Harpers Ferry at the age of 24.

Owen Brown, son of John Brown. He escaped from Harpers Ferry and died in Pasadena, California, in 1889, at the age of 65. (From the collection of Boyd B. Stutler.)

Oliver Brown, son of John Brown. He was killed at Harpers Ferry at the age of 20. Oliver married Martha Brewster in 1858. She died in the spring of 1860, at the age of 17. (From the collection of Boyd B. Stutler.)

Dangerfield Newby, who was killed at Harpers Ferry at the age of 44. He had been freed by his white father, but had a slave wife and seven slave children.

John Henri Kagi, John Brown's second in command. He was killed at Harpers Ferry at the age of 24.

John Anthony Copeland, Jr. He was a free Negro, studying in the preparatory department at Oberlin College at the time he joined John Brown. He was captured at Harpers Ferry and hanged.

The Kennedy Farmhouse in Maryland, five miles from Harpers Ferry. It was here that John Brown prepared for the raid.

Bell's two brothers, Dauphin and William Thompson, both from North Elba, had also joined John Brown's band at the farmhouse. They, too, were destined to be killed during the raid.

William Leeman, Jeremiah Anderson, Oliver and Watson Brown, whose letters have just been quoted, as well as the others, were there to fight for an ideal. But the one older man in the group, Dangerfield Newby, aged 44, had a very personal and pressing reason for being at the Kennedy farmhouse. His father, a Scotsman, married a slave, bought her, and had children by her. Though Dangerfield Newby was a free man, the curse of slavery was still hanging directly over his head. He had married a slave; Harriet, his wife, and the seven children they had begotten, were the property of a white slaveowner. Dangerfield Newby did not have the money to purchase their freedom. To Newby, the attack on Harpers Ferry was the means to rescue his wife and children.

During April, Harriet writes to him:

> You Can not imagine how much I want to see you Com as soon as you can for nothing would give me more pleasure than to see you it is the greates Comfort I have thinking of the promist time when you will be here Oh that bless hour when I shall see you once more my baby commenced to Crall today.

Then, four months later, in August, Harriet writes to her husband:

> I want you to buy me as soon as possible for if you do not get me somebody else will it is said Master is in want of monney if so I know not what time he may sell me and then all my bright hope of the future are blasted for there has been one bright hope to cheer me in all my troubles that is to be with you for if I thought I would never see you this earth would have no charms for me do all you can for me witch I have no doubt you will I want to see you so much you must write soon and say when you think you Can Come.

[107]

Hope was smashed for Harriet Newby and the little baby who "commenced to Crall," as well as the other six children, when a shot tore Newby's throat open from ear to ear during the raid on Harpers Ferry. Harriet Newby and her seven children were sold to a Louisiana slave trader.

John Brown also wrote letters during this period. As in his earlier letters during his many trips away from home, he shows his abiding concern for family and farm. On July 27, three weeks after moving into the farmhouse, he writes home to North Elba that it would be best for Watson not to set out "until sufficient hay has been secured to winter all the stock well. To be buying hay in the spring or last of the winter is ruinous."

Six weeks later, he writes:

I do not know what to advise about fattening the old spotted cow, as much will depend on what you have to feed her with; whether your heifers will come in or not next spring; also upon her present condition. You must exercise the best judgment you have in the matter, as I know but little about your crops. I should like to know more as soon as I can.

And then he adds to the desperately struggling household in North Elba: "I am now in hopes of being able to send you something in the way of help before long."

He ends this letter with one sentence to his five-year-old daughter, Ellen, the youngest of the 20 children he fathered: "Ellen, I want you to be very good."

Three weeks later, on October 1, he writes again about sending money and about the livestock:

I have encouragement of having fifty dollars or more sent you soon, to help you to get through the winter; and I shall certainly do all in my power for you, and try to commend you always to the God of my fathers.

Perhaps you can keep your animals in good condition through the winter on potatoes mostly, much cheaper than on any other feed. I think that would certainly be the case if the crop is good, and is secured well and in time.

During this time he sent an urgent plea to John Brown, Jr., to raise additional money. He writes that the shipment of freight (for which substitute the word "rifles") arrived safely, but that "the bills are very high, and I begin to be apprehensive of getting into a tight spot for want of a little more funds, notwithstanding my anxiety to make my money hold out." Then he asks if it would be possible to raise two or three hundred dollars, and suggests that his son "sound my Eastern or Western friends in regard to it." He goes on to say:

Now that arrangements are so nearly completed, I begin to feel almost certain that I can squeeze through with that amount. How I can keep my little wheels in motion for a few days more I am beginning to feel at a loss. It is terribly humiliating to me to begin soliciting of friends again; but as the harvest opens before me with increasing encouragements, I may not allow a feeling of delicacy to deter me from asking the little further aid I expect to need. I have endeavored to economize in every possible way; and I will not ask for a dollar until I am driven to do so. I have a trifle over one hundred and eighty dollars on hand, but am afraid I cannot possibly make it reach.

So great were the pressures for money that only six days before the raid, John Kagi wrote to John Brown, Jr., that the 20 men at the Kennedy farmhouse had a total of less than five dollars amongst them. On that same day, by good fortune, Francis Jackson Meriam, grandson of Francis Jackson, the great abolitionist, appeared offering both his services and his $600 inheritance.

*   *   *   *   *   *

From August 19–21 John Brown and Frederick

Douglass met in secret at an abandoned quarry near Chambersburg, Pennsylvania. Four men were present: John Brown, Frederick Douglass, John Kagi and Shields Green, an escaped slave. Of these four, the only person who remained alive to tell the story was Frederick Douglass; Kagi was killed during the raid, and both John Brown and Shields Green were hanged.

Douglass wrote an account of this meeting in his *Life And Times Of Frederick Douglass* and it will be well to look at this first:

Captain Brown, Kagi, Shields Green and myself sat down among the rocks, and talked over the enterprise. The taking of Harper's Ferry, of which Brown had merely hinted before, was now declared his settled purpose. I at once opposed it with all the arguments at my command. To me, such a measure would be fatal to running off slaves (the original plan), and fatal to all engaged. It would be an attack on the Federal Government, and would array the whole country against us. Captain Brown did not at all object to rousing the nation; it seemed to him that something startling was needed. He had completely renounced his old plan, and thought that the capture of Harper's Ferry would serve as notice to the slaves that their friends had come, and as a trumpet to rally them to his standard. I told him that all his arguments, and all his descriptions of the place convinced me that he was going into a perfect steel-trap, and that once in, he would never get out alive; he would be surrounded at once, and escape would be impossible. Our talk was long and earnest; we spent the most of Saturday and a part of Sunday in this debate—Brown for Harper's Ferry, and I against it; he for striking a blow which should instantly arouse the country, and I for the policy of gradually and unaccountably drawing off the slaves to the mountains, as at first suggested and proposed by him. When I found that he had fully made up his mind and could not be dissuaded, I turned to Green and told him he heard what Captain Brown had said—if he wished to go with me he could do so. Captain Brown urged us both to go with him. In parting, he put his arms around me in a manner more than friendly, and said, "Come with me, Douglass; I will defend you with my life. I want you for a special purpose. When I strike, the bees will begin to swarm, and I shall want you to help hive them." When about to leave, I asked Green what he had decided to do, and was surprised by his saying, in his broken way, "I b'lieve I'll go wid de ole man."

This is one of the most moving scenes in the history of our country, revealing the great cross currents of abolitionism: John Brown, white, 59, a man who had placed the fight to free the slaves before home and family, now a conspirator and outcast with a price on his head, facing Frederick Douglass, a former slave, aged 42, one of the great leaders of the Negro people and a central figure in the antislavery movement; the white man with less than four months to live, pleading with the black man to join him in an attack designed to achieve the liberation of the slave; the black man, with a span of 36 more years of fruitful life ahead of him, refusing to join, electing to advance their common cause in the way in which he was most effective—by means of his paper and speeches. Frederick Douglass realized that different strategies are proper —even more than proper, *necessary*—for different people at the same moment in history. He anticipated the physical failure of the raid, but he did not foresee the great triumph which would emanate from the failure.

(Before going further, a word about Shields Green. During the attack on Harpers Ferry, Shields Green could have escaped. Instead he decided to remain with "de ole man," even though he knew it meant certain capture and hanging.)

From Douglass's report of the meeting at the quarry, we see that John Brown wanted Douglass to "help hive" the bees when they "begin to swarm." John Brown was concerned that there be no needless violence when the slaves rose up. This concern was expressed earlier when Kagi explained to Hinton, the new recruit, the necessity for "directing and controlling the negroes, to prevent

[111]

some of the atrocities that would necessarily arise from the sudden upheaval of such a mass as the Southern slaves."

Something else was implicit in John Brown's desire to have Douglass join him. Slaves were cautious, and with justification. They knew from bitter experience the cost of being captured following an uprising. Cutting off of ears or toes, branding with hot cattle irons, being sold to the deeper South, were relatively easy punishments. Burning at the stake or public whipping until the slave died under the lash, while not frequent, did occur. The cost of joining an uprising or stampede which failed was high. Further, slaveowners had developed tactics to smoke out the more daring slave, such as falsely inducing him to join an uprising. Slaves had good reason to be suspicious; but John Brown could not afford the delay involved in overcoming their suspicion. Slaves might hesitate when approached by a white man, but this was less likely if a Frederick Douglass were to strip off his shirt and show the scars and cicatrices from the beatings he had received when he was a slave.

Frederick Douglass categorically states that he first learned of the plan to raid Harpers Ferry during the meeting at the quarry. He writes, "The taking of Harper's Ferry, of which Brown had merely hinted before, was now declared his settled purpose." He further writes, "He had completely renounced his old plan, and thought that the capture of Harper's Ferry would serve as notice to the slaves that their friends had come." The "old plan," of course, was to move directly into the mountains of Virginia without touching Harpers Ferry, and from there to make forays into the lowlands and bring the slaves to freedom via the Great Black Way. Frederick Douglass affirmed this position even earlier than in his biography, published in 1881. In a letter to Gerrit Smith, dated August 9, 1867, he wrote:

I wish to say distinctly, that John Brown never declared or

intimated to me that he was about to embark in a grand or unqualified insurrection; and that the only insurrection he proposed was the escaping of slaves, and their standing for their lives against any who should pursue them. For years before, Captain Brown's long-entertained plan was to go to the mountains in the Slave States, and to invite the slaves to flee there and stand for their freedom. His object was to make slave property unprofitable by making it insecure. Three or four weeks previous to his invasion of Harper's Ferry, Captain Brown requested me to have an interview with him at Chambersburg, Pennsylvania. I had it; and in that interview he informed me that he had determined on that invasion, instead of carrying out his old plan of going into the mountains.

This is difficult to understand. It would seem that the *one* person most likely to know John Brown's plans would be Frederick Douglass.

Such vast plans do not spring full-blown. They are the final result of a slow process of accretion; weighing, re-jecting, re-evaluating, synthesizing, until the whole slowly comes into organic focus. At some point, John Brown in-troduced Harpers Ferry into the plan and selected it as the initial target of attack. As is the nature of conspiracy, not everyone was made privy to all the details. Some were told only one part; others, different parts; a very few knew the entire plan.

There is nothing surprising about this secrecy; it is a commonplace of military operations. But I am of the opin-ion that as the plan crystallized in John Brown's mind, the one person more than any other with whom he would have conferred and taken counsel was Frederick Doug-lass. He might, and with good reason, conceal all or part of his plans from others, but not from Frederick Douglass.

Let us briefly review the relationship of John Brown and Frederick Douglass.

They met in 1847, when Douglass preached a doctrine of moral suasion, while John Brown preached that slavery was a state of war. I have already discussed their first meeting and how Douglass said of it, "My utterances became more and more tinged by the color of this man's strong impressions." They were, in fact, so strongly tinged by John Brown's doctrines that only a year and a half after their first meeting, Douglass said in a lecture in Boston:

I should welcome the intelligence tomorrow, should it come, that the slaves had risen in the South, and that the sable arms which had been engaged in beautifying and adorning the South, were engaged in spreading death and devastation.

This is quite a move away from moral suasion!

The two men interacted upon one another, with Douglass continually drawing closer to John Brown's position. During January, 1858, when John Brown needed quiet and secrecy to work on the Provisional Constitution of the Chatham Convention, it was to Douglass's home that he went. I have already quoted from Douglass's description of John Brown's stay in his house. I quote further from this description:

His whole time and thought was given to this subject. It was the first thing in the morning, and the last thing at night; till, I confess, it began to be something of a bore to me. Once in a while he would say he could, with a few resolute men, capture Harper's Ferry and supply himself with arms belonging to the Government at that place; but he never announced his intention to do so. I paid but little attention to such remarks, although I never doubted that he thought just what he said. Soon after his coming to me he asked me to get for him two smoothly planed boards, upon which he could illustrate, with a pair of dividers, by a drawing, the plan of the fortification which he meant to adopt in the mountains. These forts were to be so arranged as to connect one with the other by secret passages, so that if one was carried another could be easily fallen back upon, and be the means of dealing death to the enemy at the very

[114]

moment when he might think himself victorious. I was less interested in these drawings than my children were; but they showed that the old man had an eye to the means as well as to the end, and was giving his best thought to the work he was about to take in hand.

For Douglass to call John Brown's intense preoccupation with the subject of how to free the slaves and the forms of government to be employed when they were freed, "something of a bore," is astonishing. For Douglass to dismiss John Brown's sketches of forts with secret passages by saying, "I was less interested in these drawings than my children were," bespeaks condescension and a lack of awareness of how brilliant was this military concept. The use of secret passages and tunnels is now being effectively demonstrated in the guerrilla wars of Southeast Asia, fully 100 years after John Brown advanced their feasibility.

(Hinton confirms the concept of such forts and their use. In his book, he states that Kagi showed him plans drawn by John Brown himself for the mountain forts:

> They were to be used in ravines or "draws" when so situated that passage from one to another could be made. It was intended to conceal them by trees and thickets, place them on hillsides, and otherwise arrange them as ambuscades.)

However, the Douglass passage of most interest is the one in which he affirms that John Brown said, "he could, with a few resolute men, capture Harper's Ferry and supply himself with arms belonging to the Government at that place; but he never announced his intention to do so." In effect, what Douglass is saying is that either Harpers Ferry was not a definite part of the overall plan during January, 1858, or, if it was, that John Brown did not confide it to him.

Let us see when we first have specific information that Harpers Ferry *was* to be part of the overall plan. We know that John Brown and John Brown, Jr., visited black leaders in the Underground Railroad, including Frederick Douglass, in Philadelphia during March, 1858. In April, John Brown and his son stayed at Douglass's home in Rochester. From Rochester, John Brown went to Canada to prepare for the Chatham Convention. We know that he intended to move directly from Canada to Virginia, but that this intention was frustrated by betrayal. In order to throw everyone off the track, John Brown returned to Kansas Territory, arriving there during June, 1858. We know that he recruited Richard Hinton during the summer of 1858, and that when Kagi detailed the plan to the new recruit, it included Harpers Ferry. I quote again from Hinton's account: "Harper's Ferry was mentioned as a point to be seized, but not held,—on account of the arsenal."

Others were also being told about the plan at that time,—and the plan included Harpers Ferry. Hinton, discussing a letter which he wrote to Francis Jackson Meriam (the last of John Brown's recruits, offering both himself and his $600 inheritance), states:

> During my stay in Boston in the fall and winter of 1858, I outlined to James Redpath and Francis Jackson Meriam the plan of attack on slavery without, however, at the time naming Harper's Ferry to either of them. In a letter from Kansas to Meriam, during the spring of 1859, I told him of the point of assault.

Probably the most interesting incident—and further proof that several people knew of the inclusion of Harpers Ferry in the plan long before Frederick Douglass says it was told to him at the quarry—is the anonymous letter, dated August 20, 1859, which was sent to John B. Floyd, Secretary of War:

> I have lately received information of a movement of so great importance, that I feel it my duty to impart it to you

[116]

without delay. I have discovered the existence of a secret association, having for its object the liberation of the slaves at the South by a general insurrection. The leader of the movement is "old John Brown," late of Kansas. He has been in Canada during the winter, drilling the negroes there, and they are only waiting his word to start for the South to assist the slaves. They have one of their leading men (a white man) in an armory in Maryland,—where it is situated I have not been able to learn. As soon as everything is ready, those of their number who are in the Northern States and Canada are to come in small companies to their rendezvous, which is in the mountains of Virginia. They will pass down through Pennsylvania and Maryland, and enter Virginia at Harper's Ferry. Brown left the North about three or four weeks ago, and will arm the negroes and strike the blow in a few weeks; so that whatever is done must be done at once. They have a large quantity of arms at their rendezvous, and are probably distributing them already.

As I am not fully in their confidence, this is all the information I can give you. I dare not sign my name to this, but trust that you will not disregard the warning on that account.

For many years it was thought that this anonymous letter was written by a pro-slavery man who had stumbled onto the secret. However, when Oswald Garrison Villard was doing research in preparation for his book, *John Brown*, the author of this unsigned letter was interviewed. The letter was actually instigated by people sympathetic to John Brown, who were trying to save him and his men from the disaster they believed the attackers would suffer. The story is as follows.

You will recall that John Brown took his men to Springdale, Iowa, for training and drilling. This was, as mentioned, a village in which abolitionist Quakers had settled. While there, John Brown had confided his plans to several of these Quakers, one of whom was Moses Varney. They were given this confidence either sometime during December, 1857, when John Brown brought his men to Springdale, or during April, 1858, when he went back to

Springdale to pick up his men and take them to the Chatham Convention. The plan, as told to Moses Varney and the others, included Harpers Ferry. Varney, though active in the Underground Railroad, was yet a Quaker, and did not approve of violence.

He wrestled with this information for some time. Finally, in August, 1859, Varney unburdened himself to a friend named Smith, saying, "Something must be done to save their lives. I cannot betray their confidence in me. Consult your friends. But do something!" The "friends" in question were two brothers, by the name of Gue, then living with Smith. The three took counsel, and, finally, one of the brothers, David Gue, wrote the anonymous letter to John Floyd. David Gue later said, "Our only thought was to protect Brown from the consequences of his own rashness and devotion, without injuring him, or letting him fall into the hands of his enemies."

The men who sent the letter thought that Secretary of War Floyd would be alerted and increase the guard at the Armory in Harpers Ferry. Cook, who was the spy at Harpers Ferry, would realize that the reinforced guard meant that the plan had been betrayed and would pass this information on to John Brown. But Floyd, on his vacation at a summer resort, filed the letter away without taking action. It is indeed amazing that this man, Governor of Virginia from 1849 to 1852, sensitive to the far-reaching implications of such an attack, did nothing about the letter. Testifying before the Senate Investigating Committee referred to earlier, Floyd said:

I was satisfied in my own mind that a scheme of such wickedness and outrage could not be entertained by any citizens of the United States. I put the letter away, and thought no more of it until the raid broke out.

But my immediate interest is centered on the fact that the anonymous letter to Floyd is dated August 20, 1859, the very day that Frederick Douglass was at the quarry with John Brown.

Is it possible that Hinton was told of Harpers Ferry a full year *before* Frederick Douglass? Is it possible that peripheral figures such as Meriam, Moses Varney and others were apprised of Harpers Ferry *before* Douglass, who was so central in the fight against slavery and so close to John Brown?

* * * * * *

After the failure of the raid, John Brown's papers were found at the Kennedy farmhouse. Included was some minor correspondence with Frederick Douglass. The pro-slavery press was quick to implicate Douglass in the raid and to demand his head. In Virginia, he was immediately charged with "murder, robbery and inciting to servile insurrection." At the instigation of Governor Wise of Virginia, President Buchanan arranged for United States Marshals to try to apprehend Douglass and hand him over to Virginia.

Douglass wisely fled to Canada. Had he been delivered to Virginia, there is little question that he would not have come out alive. Writing about this during November, 1859, he said:

I have no apology for keeping out of the way of these gentlemanly United States Marshals, who are said to have paid Rochester a somewhat protracted visit lately, with a view to an interview with me. A government recognizing the Dred Scott decision at such a time as this, is not likely to have any very charitable feelings towards me. I have quite insuperable objections to being caught by the hands of Mr. Buchanan, and *"bagged"* by Gov. Wise. For this appears to be the arrangement. Buchanan does the fighting and hunting, and Wise *"bags"* the game.

I am not ashamed of endeavoring to escape from such jus-

[119]

tice as might be rationally expected by a man of color at the hands of a slaveholding court, sitting in the State of Virginia. I am not a favorite in that State, and even if acquitted by the court, with my knowledge of slaveholding magnanimity and civilization, I could scarcely hope to re-cross the slaveholding border with my life. There is no more dishonor in trying to keep out of the way of such a court, than there would be in keeping out of the way of a company of hungry wolves.

There were people who criticized Douglass for not joining John Brown in the raid. Writing about this, again during November, he said:

I am ever ready to write, speak, publish, organize, combine, and even to conspire against Slavery, when there is a reasonable hope for success. While it shall be considered right to protect oneself against thieves, burglars, robbers and assassins, and to slay a wild beast in the act of devouring his human prey, it can never be wrong for the imbruted and whip-scarred slaves, or their friends, to hunt, harass and even strike down the traffickers in human flesh. Entertaining this sentiment, I may be asked, why I did not join John Brown. My answer to this has already been given: "The tools to those that can use them." Let every man work for the abolition of Slavery in his own way. I would help all, and hinder none.

Douglass clearly understood the importance and the all-encompassing implications of the raid, despite its failure. In the November issue of his magazine, *Douglass' Monthly,* he said:

Posterity will owe everlasting thanks to John Brown and each coming generation will pay its installment of the debt.

This age is too gross and sensual to appreciate his deeds, and so calls him mad; but the future will write his epitaph upon the hearts of a people freed from slavery, because he struck the first effectual blow.

He has attacked slavery with the weapons precisely adapted to bring it to the death. Moral considerations have long since been exhausted upon slaveholders. It is in vain to reason with them. One might as well hunt bears with ethics and political economy for weapons, as to seek to "pluck the spoiled out of the hand of the oppressor" by mere force of moral law. Slavery is a system of brute force. It shields itself behind *might*, rather than right. It must be met with its own weapons. Capt. Brown has initiated a new mode of carrying on the crusade of freedom. His daring deeds may cost him his life, but the blow he has struck will, in the end, prove to be worth its mighty cost. Like Samson, he has laid his hands upon the pillars, and when he falls, that temple will speedily crumble to its final doom, burying its denizens in its ruins.

During May, 1881, Frederick Douglass delivered an address on John Brown at Storer College, located in Harpers Ferry. (It is an irony that this college, built in the very town that John Brown attacked, was founded for Negro youth soon after the close of the Civil War. It is a double irony that Douglass was invited to deliver an address in this, of all towns. It is a further irony that one of the dignitaries sitting on the platform during this address was attorney Andrew Hunter, who as we shall see, as special prosecutor for the Commonwealth of Virginia, obtained John Brown's conviction in the trial. After Frederick Douglass concluded his speech, one of the first to grasp his hand and congratulate him was attorney Andrew Hunter.) Frederick Douglass's address is a lengthy and beautifully composed piece of work. In its closing, Douglass said:

If John Brown did not end the war that ended slavery, he did at least begin the war that ended slavery. If we look over the dates, places and men, for which this honor is claimed, we shall find that not Carolina, but Virginia—not Fort Sumter, but Harper's Ferry and the arsenal—not Col. Anderson, but John Brown, began the war that ended American slavery and made this a free Republic. Until this blow was struck, the prospect for freedom was dim, shadowy and uncertain. The irrepressible conflict was one of words, votes and compromises. When John Brown stretched forth his arm the sky was cleared. The time for compromises was gone—the armed hosts of freedom stood face to face over the chasm of a broken Union—and the clash of arms was at hand.

Part IV

"A broken-winged hawk, lying on his back, with a fearless eye, and his talons set for further fight, if need be."

Governor Henry A. Wise,
The Commonwealth of Virginia.

L et us return to the Kennedy farmhouse where John Brown, about two months after his meeting with Douglass at the quarry, was making final preparations for the raid.

On October 10, six days before the raid, John Brown wrote out his first military order for the Provisional Army, General Order Number 1. In it, he detailed the organization of his army through brigade strength. The structure was conventional in design. Its smallest component was a Band, consisting of seven men headed by a corporal. A full company, including officers and men, consisted of 72; four such companies made up a battalion, totaling 288. John Brown planned to activate his units as his forces grew. However, on the day of the raid, many commissioned officers had not a single man under their command; they themselves were to serve as corporals or sergeants until their ranks were augmented.

On the same day that John Brown wrote his first military order for the Provisional Army, Kagi, in Chambersburg, wrote an interesting letter to John Brown, Jr. This letter clearly states the vast and difficult task facing John

Brown and his men. Yet implicit in Kagi's words is a quiet feeling of ultimate success:

> I shall leave here this afternoon "for good." We shall not be able to receive *any thing* from you after today. It will not do for any one to try to find us now. You must by all means keep back the men you talked of sending until you receive further instructions. Any one arriving here after today and trying to join us would be trying a very hazardous and foolish experiment. They must keep off the border until we open the way clear up to the line (M & D's) [Mason-Dixon] from the South. We will try to communicate with you as soon as possible after we strike, but it may not be possible for us to do so soon. If we succeed in getting news from the outside our own district it will be quite satisfactory, but we have not the most distant hopes it will be possible for us to receive *recruits for weeks*, or quite likely *months* to come. We must first make a complete and indisputably open road to the free states. That will require both labor and time.

We owe our knowledge of the last day at the Kennedy farmhouse to the first-hand accounts of John Cook and Osborne Perry Anderson. Cook, captured and sentenced to be hanged, wrote his account in prison. Anderson, a free Canadian Negro, by trade a printer, succeeded in escaping from Harpers Ferry. Subsequently, he wrote *A Voice From Harper's Ferry*. In it, he says:

> On Sunday, October the 16th, Captain Brown arose earlier than usual and called his men to worship. He read a chapter from the Bible applicable to the condition of the slaves and our duty as their brethren, and then offered up a fervent prayer to God to assist us in the liberation of the bondsmen.

For the benefit of those who had not yet heard it, the Provisional Constitution was read. John Brown administered the oath to those who had not yet taken it. Kagi wrote out official commissions for the appointed officers. During the afternoon, John Brown wrote 11 military

[124]

orders. These detailed the plan of attack and the exact sequence in which the steps were to be carried out.

The entire army consisted of 21 men: 16 white, five black. The men were given their final instructions. In closing, according to Cook's narrative, John Brown said:

> And now, gentlemen, let me press this one thing upon your minds. You all know how dear life is to you, and how dear your lives are to your friends; and, in remembering that, consider that the lives of others are as dear to them as yours are to you; do not, therefore, take the life of anyone if you can possibly avoid it, but if it is necessary to take life in order to save your own, then make sure work of it.

At about eight o'clock that evening, John Brown ordered, "Men, get on your arms; we will proceed to the Ferry." John Brown and 18 men started down to Harpers Ferry. Three men were detailed to remain behind to guard arms and supplies. John Brown intended to send a wagon back to the farmhouse for this material as soon as he had control of Harpers Ferry.

The Kennedy farmhouse was (and still is) situated in the hills of Maryland, about five miles from the Virginia border. To enter Harpers Ferry, it was necessary to cross a covered bridge which spanned the Potomac. Harpers Ferry is situated at the confluence of the Potomac and Shenandoah Rivers. It was then a prosperous town of about 3,000 inhabitants whose livelihood revolved around the Rifle Works and Federal Armory.

The Armory and Arsenal were at the water's edge, a fair distance away from the town proper, in what might be called the extreme downtown section. The two bridges, one spanning the Potomac, the other the Shenandoah, were quite near each other. Except for the Rifle Works about half a mile away, the area in which John Brown had chosen to operate was no more than a few hundred yards.

When John Brown and his 18 men neared Harpers

Ferry, two men, the vanguard, cut the telegraph wires. The men reached the covered bridge at about ten o'clock. The unsuspecting watchman on the bridge was taken prisoner. Two men remained to guard the bridge, while the others, taking the watchman with them, entered Virginia and quickly proceeded to the Armory, a short distance before them.

With a crowbar, they broke the chains, opened the gate and seized the Armory watchman. Acting under John Brown's military orders, two men were dispatched to the Shenandoah Bridge and seized it; two men moved quickly to the Rifle Works, captured its guard, and took control of the building; two men entered the Arsenal, which was across the way from the Armory, and occupied it. The prisoners who had been captured at all the points were delivered under guard to the Armory. There they discovered other prisoners, townspeople captured in the streets. Throughout the early hours of the morning, prisoners were delivered to the Armory. In all, it is estimated that John Brown captured about 50 prisoners whom he intended to use as hostages or in exchange for slaves.

Before midnight, John Brown had control of the two bridges, the Armory, the Arsenal and the Rifle Works. His prisoners outnumbered his total force. All this had been accomplished in the space of two hours and without the firing of a single bullet. Surely, these first hours are a classic example of a brilliantly executed commando raid!

One of the military orders which John Brown had written that afternoon reads:

That Captain A. D. Stevens proceed to the country with his men, and after taking certain parties prisoners, bring them to the Ferry. In the case of Colonel Lewis Washington, who had certain arms in his possession, he must, after being secured as a prisoner, deliver them into the hands of Osborne P. Anderson. Anderson being a colored man, and colored men being only *things* in the South, it is proper that the South be taught a lesson upon this point.

The background and meaning of this order is as follows: John Brown had sent Cook to Harpers Ferry several months ahead of the others in order to spy out the land. Cook took a job as lock-tender on the canal and on the side he peddled books. Thus, he had the opportunity to scout the area and make notes about the households, their occupants, number of slaves, arms possessed, and other pertinent details. During the course of his scouting, he devised an opportunity to visit the home of Colonel Lewis Washington, great grandnephew of George Washington and military aide to Governor Wise of Virginia.

At Colonel Washington's home, Cook was shown a pair of pistols which Lafayette had presented to George Washington, and also a sword which, according to tradition, had been presented to George Washington by Frederick the Great. These had descended to Colonel Lewis Washington. John Brown, always aware of the value of such symbols and the uses to which they could be put, ordered that when captured, Colonel Washington must place sword and pistols into the hands of a Negro.

And so it was. The party left Harpers Ferry for Colonel Washington's house around midnight and arrived there at about half-past one. The house was broken into; Colonel Washington was made prisoner and forced to deliver the historic sword and pistols into the hands of Osborne Anderson.

This was indeed a dramatic scene: the room lit by a pine torch; Colonel Washington awakened out of his slumber in the middle of the night suddenly faced with armed men, white and Negro, being informed that he was a prisoner, that his slaves were to be freed, and that he must place his valued family treasures into the hands of a Negro. Surely Lewis Washington felt the foundation of his society shaking that night—the precursor to the upheaval less than two years away.

Three or four of Colonel Washington's slaves were released, and his great farm wagon, which had a span of four horses, taken. On the way back to Harpers Ferry, the party stopped off at the home of another wealthy farmer, John H. Allstadt, who with his son was made prisoner; seven of his slaves were liberated and taken along.

At about three in the morning, the wagon, now loaded with about 20 people, arrived at the Armory. At the Congressional Committee, Colonel Lewis Washington described his first meeting with John Brown:

> He came and said, "I presume you are Mr. Washington. It is too dark to see to write at this time, but when it shall have cleared off a little and become lighter, I shall require you to write to some of your friends to send a stout able-bodied negro; I think after a while, possibly, I shall be enabled to release you, but only on the condition of getting your friends to send in a negro as a ransom. My particular reason for taking you first was that, as the aid to the governor of Virginia, I knew you would endeavor to perform your duty, and perhaps you would have been a troublesome customer to me; and apart from that, I wanted you particularly for the moral effect it would give our cause, having one of your name as a prisoner."

By five o'clock in the morning, this huge wagon with its four horses was on the way to the Kennedy farmhouse. In the wagon were John Cook, several of the men, and, according to Osborne Anderson's account, 14 released slaves. (Cook's account says four slaves.) Their instructions were to bring the arms and supplies from the farmhouse to a schoolhouse about a mile outside Harpers Ferry. When it was time to make a break for the mountains, the equipment would be brought into Harpers Ferry and consolidated with whatever arms John Brown took from the Armory and the Arsenal.

In point of fact, none of the arms collected with such enormous difficulty ever reached the men in Harpers Ferry. Until the end, they were forced to fight with only the arms they had carried with them when they crossed the bridge.

Harpers Ferry in 1859. The covered bridge is in the foreground; the Potomac River is to the right and the Shenandoah River is to the left. The Kennedy farmhouse in Maryland is in the hills at the extreme right. The United States Armory is the series of low buildings with the smokestack, along the Potomac River. (Courtesy Baltimore and Ohio Railroad.)

The United States Armory at Harpers Ferry is the series of buildings to the right. The Fire Engine house where John Brown and his men made their last stand is the corner building on the left.

United States Marines under the command of Brevet-Colonel Robert E. Lee storming the Fire Engine house, October 18, 1859.

John Brown and his men defend the Fire Engine house.

United States Marines batter the door of the Fire Engine house.

The first shot was fired at midnight. The Potomac Bridge had two watchmen. The second of these arrived at midnight to relieve the first, by then a prisoner. This second watchman was ordered to halt. Instead, he started to flee. A bullet was fired which creased his scalp, but did no permanent damage. The watchman ran to the nearby hotel, the Wager House, to spread the alarm. Surprisingly, nothing happened. Several people went out to see what was going on and quickly moved back into the safety of the lobby.

At about 1:30 in the morning, another shot was fired. Hayward Shepherd, a free Negro employed as a porter at the railroad depot, was ordered to halt but refused to do so. He started to run and was shot. He died that day of his wounds. It is a tragic and ironic comment that the first casualty was a free Negro.

With the firing of this second bullet, a new factor entered the situation. Soon the Lutheran church bell was rung, warning the people that something was amiss. Of those who heard the bell, few responded; if anything, the ringing served to keep most home on this wet, cold night. However, despite the cold and the rain, slowly and sporadically a few townspeople began to gather. Though John Brown would have absolute control of Harpers Ferry for another nine to ten hours, the weight of the situation had begun to shift against him; slowly he began to lose the advantage gained by his surprise attack.

Bits and pieces of information were beginning to spread, but no one in this town of 3,000, rudely awakened in the middle of the night, had any notion of what was *really* happening. There was a rumor that the vaults in the Federal Government Armory had been sacked and the gold looted. Some thought that these outsiders were involved in a strike against the railroad. But when the townspeople saw that some of the outsiders were Negroes, and also observed with alarm the profusion of arms, they knew that something beyond a mere railroad strike was taking place. Rumors circulated and grew in retelling. The invaders were credited with numbering 150, then with being 600–700 strong; later this grew to an attacking force of 1500 heavily-armed men.

One of the townspeople, scouting around the fringes of the Armory and seeing prisoners being brought in there at a goodly rate, realized that something critical was going on. He mounted his horse and raced in the night to the nearby town of Charlestown, arriving early in the morning. The volunteer military organization, the Jefferson Guard, was quickly mustered and loaded onto a train for Harpers Ferry. During the day, volunteer organizations from Martinsburg, Shepherdstown and a few other towns also began to converge on Harpers Ferry.

Meanwhile, some of the townspeople returned to their homes for weapons. It is another irony that in this town where there were tens of thousands of rifles, the inhabitants themselves were poorly armed. They had only fowling pieces, some squirrel guns, an occasional rifle. Not until later that day were they able to get at the Armory rifles.

By dawn a handful of men had taken positions in buildings a respectful distance away from the Armory. The rest of the sleeping town soon awoke to the sound of firing. Although the exchange of fire began soon after dawn, it was sporadic and John Brown was still in control of Harpers Ferry. He could have withdrawn at any time that morning of Monday, October 17, and still have achieved a substantial, though partial, victory. Slaves had developed secret means of extremely rapid communication; within a matter of days, news of the raid and of John Brown's army in the mountains could have reached the slaves in plantations of the deep South. The history of slave revolts and stampedes, and of equal importance the history of the thousands of slaves who had already fled to the North, indicates that many would have been ready to throw off their yoke upon learning that the raid was successful and that a guerrilla force was operating in the mountains.

Throughout the morning, Kagi and Stevens urged John Brown to gather his forces scattered at the two bridges, the Arsenal, the Rifle Works, and withdraw. But John Brown held fast and by this decision committed a fatal error.

In good part, he stood ground because of the fact that the men who had taken Colonel Washington's wagon and horses up to the Kennedy farmhouse had not returned. John Brown had assigned this large a proportion of his entire force to convey the arms and supplies from the farm to the schoolhouse because it was of paramount importance that this be done rapidly. This move, which should have taken only a few hours, took about ten. The men charged with the task wasted the hours unconscionably. They finished their mission at about four o'clock that afternoon. It was then too late; they were cut off from Harpers Ferry because the bridge over the Potomac had already been taken by the Jefferson Guards who had appeared on the Maryland side of the Potomac Bridge about noon.

The prospect of losing so many men and hard-won arms and supplies was a shattering one for John Brown. The alternative was to remain in Harpers Ferry and run the risk of the enemy overwhelming him. John Brown had once advised the League of Gileadites to strike unexpectedly, get the job done and then rapidly disengage from the enemy before their superior numbers could be brought into play. By electing to remain in Harpers Ferry, he was now guilty of transgressing his own advice. For this transgression he was to pay a heavy price. The Jefferson Guard had retaken the bridge, driving off the four or five men defending it. During this encounter, Dangerfield Newby, husband to a slave and father of seven slave children, was shot and killed. He was the first of John Brown's men to

[131]

die. It is, once again, a tragic and ironic comment that the first casualties on both sides were Negroes: Hayward Shepherd and Dangerfield Newby.

Soon after the taking of the bridge over the Potomac, the Shenandoah Bridge was also cut off. John Brown's defeat was now a matter of time.

With the capture of the Potomac Bridge, John Brown and the few men he had with him retreated first into the Armory grounds, and then further into the Fire Engine house located on the Federal Government compound. He used the Fire Engine house as a fortress; it is here that he made his last stand. He was joined by the men driven off the two bridges; but the men assigned to the Kennedy farmhouse, those at the Rifle Works and those at the Arsenal, were cut off from him and isolated from each other—a dispersal of forces which made it relatively easy for the opposing force to overpower him.

When John Brown retreated into the Fire Engine house, he took with him the more important hostages, including Colonel Washington and John Allstadt. There the prisoners stayed, throughout that long day and into the next morning, until they were rescued. Without exception they testified to John Brown's concern for their safety. He had placed them farthest away from the windows where they were least likely to be hit by the bullets fired into the building.

During the afternoon, attempts were made to establish a truce. John Brown sent out one of his men for a parley. Although this man carried a white flag, he was seized, dragged out on the bridge, shot, and shoved through the trestle into the shallow water. There, his body was used for target practice.

Later in the day, another parley was attempted. Two men, one of them Watson Brown, went out carrying a

[132]

flag of truce. Both were shot down. Watson was able to drag himself back to the fortress; he died of his wounds the next day. (Oliver was also shot that day, and died during the night.)

John Brown was incensed at the killing of men bearing a white flag, yet he treated his prisoners with courtesy and consideration. Years later, one of the prisoners in the Fire Engine house, relating his experiences with John Brown, wrote:

> I was a witness at the trial. I could not go to see him hanged. He had made me a prisoner, but had spared my life and that of other gentlemen in his power; and when his sons were shot down beside him, almost any other man similarly placed would at least have exacted life for life.

The Provisional Constitution had stipulated that all prisoners be treated with respect and kindness. John Brown followed his own tenets.

By late afternoon, militia and volunteer guards from nearby towns, as well as citizens from Harpers Ferry and the outlying districts, had gathered; in all, close to a thousand men. Though the ultimate outcome was inevitable, these thousand men were held off hour after hour by the half-dozen men in the Fire Engine house.

President Buchanan and Secretary of War Floyd had received word that Harpers Ferry was occupied by an invading force of at least 700 Negroes and whites. Accordingly, they dispatched a company of United States Marines. It is interesting to note that this company consisted of only 90 men and two officers—the entire military force in all of Washington that weekend!

The 92 Marines were placed under the command of Brevet-Colonel Robert E. Lee, who was assisted by First Lieutenant J. E. B. Stuart. At around midnight, they entered Harpers Ferry. Colonel Lee determined to end the battle as rapidly as possible. Concerned for the prisoners held by John Brown, he decided not to engage in rifle fire.

[133]

He immediately made preparations to rush the Fire Engine house at dawn and engage the enemy at close quarters with bayonet and sword.

With the first light, Lieutenant J. E. B. Stuart approached the Fire Engine house with an order to surrender. John Brown refused. Colonel Lee ordered the attack. A nearby ladder was used as a battering ram; a hole was smashed through the door; the Marines stormed in; the charge was over in three minutes.

Here, a digression for a moment.

It is generally accepted that the slaves did not rise up and join John Brown, and this is advanced as proof that they were too timid or cowardly to do so. Or, as the South liked to have it, this indicated that the vast majority of slaves were content to remain as they were. In a speech given three days after John Brown's capture, Governor Wise said:

> The faithful slaves refused to take up arms against their masters; and those who were taken by force from their happy homes deserted their liberators as soon as they could dare to make the attempt. Not a slave around us was found faithless.

Perhaps Governor Wise and his fellow Virginians took comfort in the notion that slaves would not desert their "happy homes." But the thousands of slaves fleeing to the North each year and the necessity for the South to maintain constant semimilitary patrols speak otherwise.

The facts of the Civil War also speak otherwise. Two hundred thousand blacks joined the Union Army; one hundred thousand of them were slaves. Thirty thousand enlisted in the Navy. Herbert Aptheker, in his *A Documentary History of the Negro People in the United States* notes, "Another quarter of a million Negro men and

The Louisiana Colored Volunteers at Port Hudson, Louisiana, May 27, 1863. The first major engagement of Negro troops in the Civil War. (From the New York Public Library, Schomburg Collection.)

54th Massachusetts Colored Regiment at the charge on Fort Wagner, South Carolina, July 18, 1863. (From the Library of Congress, Prints and Photographs.)

women labored for that Army and Navy as teamsters, nurses, cooks, pilots, fortification-builders and pioneers, while many more served as guides, spies and scouts." What is more, during the first period of the Civil War, the North refused the services of blacks as soldiers. In order to join, they had to carry on an extensive campaign. Aptheker's book presents many stirring documents which show the black man's determination to be allowed to enter the army and fight for the Union. Thus, every Negro in the Union Army was a volunteer who was there because of intense conviction. Their valor in combat was attested to by their officers. So important was their contribution that President Lincoln stated that without their service, the struggle would have had to be abandoned in three weeks. After the war, Edwin M. Stanton, Secretary of War, stated: "The whole contest would have gone against us if we had not got 200,000 negroes to come and join our armies and turn the tide of victory on our side."

Then why didn't the slaves in the area around Harpers Ferry join the raid, as is generally testified?

In the first place, there is evidence to show that John Brown found it necessary to advance the date of his raid by approximately 10 days. Osborne Perry Anderson, in his *A Voice From Harper's Ferry* writes:

> Could other parties, waiting for the word, have reached the headquarters in time for the outbreak when it took place, the taking of the armory, engine-house, and rifle factory, would have been quite different. But the men at the farm had been so closely confined, that they went out about the house and farm in the daytime during that week, and so indiscreetly exposed their numbers to the prying neighbors, who thereupon took steps to have a search instituted in the early part of the coming week.

At best, it was difficult to get word to the slave quarters. If the bolder and stronger slaves had been informed of a date which was suddenly changed to 10 days earlier, they would have been caught unawares. By the time the information *had* seeped through to them, it was too late; John Brown was trapped in Harpers Ferry. Further, they would have had good reason to be suspicious if they were told that the raid was taking place at that very moment; it might be a ruse to smoke them out. Prudence and wisdom dictated that they hold back until they could ascertain the facts.

And certainly it can be assumed that the moment a slave master learned of the raid, he put his slaves under close guard.

Secondly, there is evidence which shows that in addition to the slaves who were liberated by John Brown's men, a number voluntarily joined him. Osborne Perry Anderson, a member of the party that went to Colonel Lewis Washington's house, wrote further:

On the road we met some colored men, to whom we made known our purpose, when they immediately agreed to join us. They said they had been long waiting for an opportunity of the kind. Stevens then asked them to go around among the colored people and circulate the news. The result was that many colored men gathered to the scene of action.

Of the various contradictory reports made by the slaveholders and their satellites about the time of the Harper's Ferry conflict, none were more untruthful than those relating to the slaves. There was seemingly a studied attempt to enforce the belief that the slaves were cowardly, and that they were really more in favor of Virginia masters and slavery, than of their freedom. As a party who had an intimate knowledge of the conduct of the colored men engaged, I am prepared to make an emphatic denial of the gross imputation against them.

There is no way of knowing how many slaves actually gathered, nor is there any way of knowing how many of them participated in the action. My personal evaluation is that a goodly number of them stood by, waiting to see how successful the raid would be and what further steps John Brown would take before they would commit themselves. When they saw that the raid was a failure, they returned to their masters' farms as quickly as they could, figuratively fading into the landscape.

Over the years, all oppressed people develop techniques for survival. To survive in this particular instance meant slaves must get back to their masters' farms, pretend ignorance and be unusually docile.

The South as a matter of policy always toned down or suppressed news of slave insurgence. Word to the public about any break for freedom was not desirable. Even in so resounding an event as John Brown's raid on Harpers Ferry, the South maintained this policy. However, an attentive reading of the documents shows that slaves did join in the raid and it also relates the fate of those who were caught.

Two examples will suffice.

When Colonel Washington testified before the Congressional Committee mentioned earlier, the following colloquy took place:

Question: How many of your negroes did they take, including your house servants?

Washington: My servants were almost all away, that being Sunday night. They took two of mine, and one, the husband of one of my servants.

Question: Did they take but three negro men of yours, altogether?

Washington: Only three there. One other heard something was wrong, and got in the wagon at Allstadt's. I understand that was the point where he overtook them. That man who joined them at Allstadt's did not belong to me, but to Dr. Fuller. He was hired at my house.

This testimony presents us with an interesting picture. Notice, first, that although Colonel Washington euphemistically refers to his slaves as "servants," the harsh reality of their lives is quite apparent. One of the women slaves has a husband who is allowed to visit her on Sunday—provided his master gives him permission to do so. Next, we see that Colonel Washington hired a slave from a Dr. Fuller and that this slave, hearing news of what was going on, chased after the wagon and overtook it at the Allstadt's farm. (Allstadt's was the second stop for Stevens's party. Here they took Allstadt and his son as hostages, and also liberated seven slaves.) Notice, too, with what delicate euphemism Colonel Washington describes how Dr. Fuller's slave joined Stevens's party: "One other heard something was wrong, and got in the wagon at Allstadt's."

The testimony goes on. Four and a half pages later, we find further information about Dr. Fuller's slave:

Question: Did you get back all your slaves?
Washington: Yes, sir; except the servant that was drowned at Hall's works. [Hall's works referred to is the rifle factory.] The others made their escape from those men who armed them, and were at home when I got there. They must have gone back on Tuesday night, I imagine. I did not go back until Wednesday evening. I remained at the Ferry with the Governor two days.
Question: Did you find your negroes at home when you went back?
Washington: Yes, sir.
Question: You lost none of your negroes?
Washington: No, sir.
Question: But a man whom you hired from Dr. Fuller was drowned in the canal?
Washington: Yes, sir.
Question: Did it excite any spirit of insubordination amongst your negroes?
Washington: Not the slightest. If anything, they were much more tractable than before.

It is interesting that Dr. Fuller's slave, who had run

after the wagon to join John Brown's men, was later found drowned in the canal.

John Allstadt's exchange with the members of the Congressional Committee is equally interesting:

Question: Did you get all your negroes back?
Allstadt: All but one.
Question: What became of him?
Allstadt: He was taken to Charlestown to the jail.
Question: What ultimately became of him?
Allstadt: He died.
Question: How? From what cause?
Allstadt: I do not know. He was frightened very much, I suppose, and exposed very much that day; it was a very bad day; it rained very hard; I suppose he was exposed to the rain and cold; he was taken sick after he had been in jail a few days, and died.
Question: Then your negroes all got home that night, except one who was taken to Charlestown?
Allstadt: Yes, sir.
Question: Did you see him in jail?
Allstadt: Yes, sir; I took cold in the engine-house. I was very hoarse when I came out of the engine-house on Tuesday; I thought I had better take care of myself, or else I might be taken sick; I did not go to Charlestown for some few days; I do not know how long; I saw the negro there when I went; he was very sick when I went there, so much so that I could not move him home.
Question: Do you know why he was taken to jail?
Allstadt: I inquired, and they said they did not know they had committed him to jail; the magistrate had committed him to jail, and I would see further about him when I went to town.
Question: Did you hear of any charges being made against him?
Allstadt: No, sir.
Question: The negro died from sickness in jail?
Allstadt: Yes, sir; he was too sick to carry home.

[139]

Question: What was his age?

Allstadt: He was about twenty years old. He was a very valuable fellow; the most valuable one I had.

Here we are asked to believe that John Allstadt, for fear that he "might be taken sick," put off the trip to Charlestown for several days even though his farm was but a few miles away. We are further asked to believe that Allstadt did not see fit to send anyone else in his place, that he did not even hire a lawyer to find out why his most valuable slave had been jailed without a charge. Allstadt knew that his slave had been exposed to the rain and cold as he had been that day and night, and probably was as sick as he, yet, according to his statement, he did nothing to protect his property, letting him languish in jail until he died.

The name of the slave referred to was Phil, and it was given out directly after the raid that he died of a combination of fright and exposure. Allstadt, in his sworn testimony before the Congressional Committee, affirms this allegation. However, Osborne Perry Anderson in his *A Voice From Harper's Ferry,* published one year after Allstadt's testimony, has a totally different story to tell about Phil:

> As in the war of the American Revolution, the first blood shed was a black man's, Crispus Attucks, so at Harper's Ferry, the first blood shed by our party, after the arrival of the United States troops, was that of a slave. In the beginning of the encounter, and before the troops had fairly emerged from the bridge a slave was shot. I saw him fall. Phil, the slave who died in prison, with fear, as it was reported, was wounded at the Ferry, and died from the effects of it.

It has long been the practice to eliminate intractables by incarcerating them, and if wounded or ill, letting them die of neglect. I suggest that Allstadt's slave, Phil, was killed off in precisely this way.

One further point needs discussion before we resume the main thread of the story. It is often advanced that, in addition to the error of striking at a militarily untenable position, John Brown did not take into account the composition of the population around Harpers Ferry. Harpers Ferry was farming country, not plantation land, and had very few slaves. In the deep South where the plantations were located, there was a heavy concentration of slaves, but further north, near Harpers Ferry, there was only a handful of slaves scattered here and there on the wealthier farms. In addition, the living conditions of a farm slave around Harpers Ferry were considerably easier than the brutal life of a plantation slave. Thus, it is argued, John Brown could not expect a general uprising of slaves.

In answer: John Brown did not expect, nor did he desire, a general uprising. At the interrogation after his capture—which I will shortly describe—he was asked, "Did you expect a general uprising of the slaves in case of your success?" He answered, "No, sir, nor did I wish it. I expected to gather them from time to time and set them free."

John Brown spoke truly. He was not interested in insurrection; he *was* interested in laying out the structure for a guerrilla movement. A general uprising would have been a catastrophe for him because he was not equipped to handle the logistics of organizing for the sustenance and training of large numbers. The value of Harpers Ferry was the Armory and the Arsenal. It was a means of joining the issue—forcibly, irretrievably, and on a national scale. He saw it as a means of informing both the Southern slave and the Northern sympathizer of the existence of his guerrilla force in the mountains. But he did not expect, nor wish, a large uprising.

Let us now go back to the storming of the Fire Engine house by the United States Marines. After John Brown

[141]

and his men were overpowered, the dead and wounded were laid out on the grass. Of the 11 who had retreated into the Fire Engine house, six were dead, three were wounded, two were unharmed—though they were soon to be hanged.

John Brown, suffering sword cuts on head, neck and shoulders, and sword thrusts that reached to his kidney, was carried to the paymaster's room in the Armory. There he was laid on the floor on what the reporter for the *New York Herald* described as "miserable shakedowns, covered with some old bedding."

At about noon Governor Wise came in from Richmond. He and a host of officials immediately went into the paymaster's room to interrogate John Brown. In Governor Wise's entourage were Senator James M. Mason, who had introduced the Fugitive Slave Law in the Senate, Representative Clement L. Vallandigham of Ohio, ex-Representative Charles Faulkner of Virginia, and attorney Andrew Hunter, who would be John Brown's prosecutor at the trial. Present also were Colonel Robert E. Lee, Colonel Lewis Washington, Lieutenant J. E. B. Stuart. Other notables, as well as ordinary citizens, crowded into the room. But the most important people in that room were several newspaper reporters; they telegraphed the details of this interrogation to their papers, and thus to the nation. The telegraph had recently come into its own. The raid on Harpers Ferry, John Brown's trial and the hanging following it, were probably the first stories ever to receive daily national coverage. It is one of the many ironies of the events at Harpers Ferry that the *New York Herald*, a major newspaper and strongly pro-slavery, was the main source from which the entire nation learned of this interview.

If ever a man had the right to close his eyes and turn away from the world, it was this 59-year-old John Brown. His raid was a disaster; 20 years of planning, effort and sacrifice were in the dust; one son was dead, another dying; and he, wounded and bleeding, was on the floor encircled by his enemies. He had not slept for approximately 60 hours, nor eaten for about 48. The reporter from *Harper's Weekly* described John Brown thus:

His hair was a mass of clotted gore, so that I could not distinguish the original color; his eye a pale blue or gray, nose Roman, and beard (originally sandy) white and blood-stained.

Colonel Lee, who by order of President Buchanan was in command, offered to exclude visitors if they annoyed him. The *New York Herald* reporter wrote: "Brown said he was by no means annoyed; on the contrary he was glad to be able to make himself and his motives clearly understood."

The reporter from the Baltimore *American* wrote:

In the midst of his enemies, whose home he had invaded, wounded and a prisoner, surrounded by a small army of officials, and a more desperate army of angry men; with the gallows staring him full in the face, he lay on the floor, and, in reply to every question, gave answers that betokened the spirit that animated him.

The interrogation lasted more than three hours. The sword and the word! It seemed as though the sword which was wrested from his hand at Harpers Ferry was now to be transformed into the word. He became the accuser; his interrogators, the accused. Yet something else was involved. John Brown was absolutely determined to embrace and carry with him the enemy. In effect, he was saying: "My moral superiority is going to conquer your immoral conviction—somehow! And if I cannot conquer, then my moral strength will neutralize you—somehow!"

The long interrogation began. There were hundreds of questions. At first, his questioners tried to find out who his supporters were, with a view to implicating them politically. But John Brown soon took the platform away from his enemies and directed the interrogation to the issue of slavery:

Senator Mason:	If you would tell us who sent you here,—who provided the means,—that would be information of some value.
John Brown:	I will answer freely and faithfully about what concerns myself,—I will answer anything I can with honor,—but not about others.
Congressman Vallandigham:	Mr. Brown, who sent you here?
John Brown:	No man sent me here; it was my own prompting and that of my Maker, or that of the Devil,—whichever you please to ascribe it to. I acknowledge no master in human form.
Vallandigham:	Did you get up the expedition yourself?
John Brown:	I did.
Vallandigham:	Did you get up this document that is called a Constitution?
John Brown:	I did.
Mason:	How many are there engaged with you in this movement?
John Brown:	Any questions that I can honorably answer I will,—not otherwise. So far as I am myself concerned, I have told you everything truthfully. I value my word, sir.
Mason:	What was your object in coming?
John Brown:	We came to free slaves, and only that.
A Volunteer:	How many men, in all, had you?
John Brown:	I came to Virginia with eighteen men only, beside myself.
Volunteer:	What in the world did you suppose you could do here in Virginia with that amount of men?
John Brown:	Young man, I do not wish to discuss that question here.
Mason:	How do you justify your acts?

[144]

John Brown:	I think, my friend, you are guilty of a great wrong against God and humanity,—I say it without wishing to be offensive,—and it would be perfectly right for any one to interfere with you so far as to free those you wilfully and wickedly hold in bondage. I do not say this insultingly.
Mason:	I understand that.
John Brown:	I think I did right, and that others will do right who interfere with you at any time and at all times. I hold that the Golden Rule, "Do unto others as ye would that others should do unto you" applies to all who would help others to gain their liberty.
Lt. Stuart:	But you don't believe in the Bible.
John Brown:	Certainly I do.
Mason:	Did you consider this a military organization in this Constitution? I have not yet read it.
John Brown:	I did, in some sense. I wish you would give that paper close attention.
Mason:	You consider yourself the commander-in-chief of these "provisional" military forces?
John Brown:	I was chosen, agreeably to the ordinance of a certain document, commander-in-chief of that force.
Mason:	What wages did you offer?
John Brown:	None.
Stuart:	"The wages of sin is death."
John Brown:	I would not have made such a remark to you if you had been a prisoner, and wounded, in my hands.
A Bystander:	Do you consider this a religious movement?
John Brown:	It is, in my opinion, the greatest service man can render to God.
Bystander:	Do you consider yourself an instrument in the hands of Providence?
John Brown:	I do.

[145]

Bystander:	Upon what principle do you justify your acts?
John Brown:	Upon the Golden Rule. I pity the poor in bondage that have none to help them; that is why I am here; not to gratify any personal animosity, revenge, or vindictive spirit. It is my sympathy with the oppressed and wronged, that are as good as you and as precious in the sight of God.
Vallandigham:	Who are your advisors in this movement?
John Brown:	I cannot answer that. I want you to understand, gentlemen, [and then he said to the reporter of the *New York Herald*, "You may report that."]—I want you to understand that I respect the rights of the poorest and weakest of colored people, oppressed by the slave system, just as much as I do those of the most wealthy and powerful. This is the idea that has moved me, and that alone. We expected no reward except the satisfaction of endeavoring to do for those in distress and greatly oppressed as we would be done by. The cry of distress of the oppressed is my reason, and the only thing that prompted me to come here. Moral suasion is hopeless. I don't think the people of the slave states will ever consider the subject of slavery in its true light till some other argument is resorted to than moral suasion.
Reporter:	I do not wish to annoy you; but if you have anything further you would like to say, I will report it.
John Brown:	I have nothing to say, only that I claim to be here in carrying out a measure I believe perfectly justifiable, and not to act the part of an incendiary or ruffian, but to aid those suffering great wrong. I wish to say, furthermore, that you had better—all of you people at the South—prepare

yourselves for a settlement of that question that must come up for settlement sooner than you are prepared for it. The sooner you are prepared the better. You may dispose of me very easily,—I am nearly disposed of now; but this question is still to be settled,—this negro question, I mean; the end of that is not yet.

Question: Brown, suppose you had every nigger in the United States, what would you do with them?

John Brown: Set them free.

A Bystander: To set them free would sacrifice the life of every man in this community.

John Brown: I do not think so.

Bystander: I know it. I think you are fanatical.

John Brown: And I think you are fanatical. "Whom the gods would destroy they first make mad," and you are mad.

A Bystander: Robber!

John Brown: You are the robbers.

Governor Wise: Mr. Brown, the silver of your hair is reddened by the blood of crime, and you should eschew these hard words and think upon eternity. You are suffering from wounds, perhaps fatal; and should you escape death from these causes, you must submit to a trial which may involve death. Your confessions justify the presumption that you will be found guilty; and even now you are committing a felony under the laws of Virginia, by uttering sentiments like these. It is better you should turn your attention to your eternal future than be dealing in denunciations which can only injure you.

John Brown: Governor, I have, from all appearances, not more than fifteen or twenty years the start of you in the journey to that eternity of which you kindly warn me; and whether my tenure here shall be fifteen

[147]

months, or fifteen days, or fifteen hours, I am equally prepared to go. There is an eternity behind and an eternity before, and the little speck in the centre, however long, is but comparatively a minute. The difference between your tenure and mine is trifling, and I therefore tell you to be prepared; I am prepared. You all have a heavy responsibility, and it behooves you to prepare more than it does me.

Governor Wise described John Brown as "a broken-winged hawk, lying on his back, with a fearless eye, and his talons set for further fight, if need be."

And later, when John Brown was accused of being mad, Governor Wise said:

They are themselves mistaken who take him to be a madman. He is a bundle of the best nerves I ever saw; cut and thrust and bleeding, and in bonds. He is a man of clear head, of courage, fortitude, and simple ingenuousness. He is cool, collected, and indomitable, and it is but just to him to say that he was humane to his prisoners, and he inspired me with great trust in his integrity as a man of truth. Colonel Washington says that he was the coolest and firmest man he ever saw in defying danger and death. With one son dead by his side, and another shot through, he felt the pulse of his dying son with one hand, held his rifle with the other, and commanded his men with the utmost composure, encouraging them to be firm, and to sell their lives as dearly as they could.

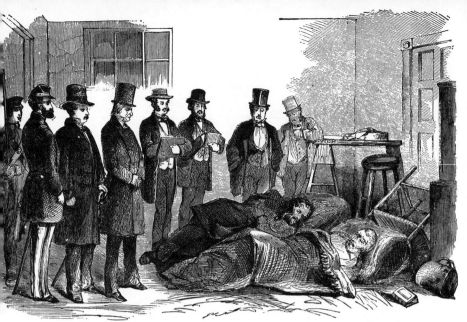

John Brown and Aaron Stevens are interrogated on October 18, 1859, by Governor Wise of Virginia, Senator Mason and others. Two reporters are present. (Frank Leslie's Illustrated Paper, October 29, 1859. Artist: Alfred Berghaus.)

Governor Henry A. Wise of Virginia at the time of the raid. He became a Brigadier-General in the Confederate Army. (From the collection of Boyd B. Stutler.)

Andrew Hunter, prosecuting attorney in John Brown's trial.

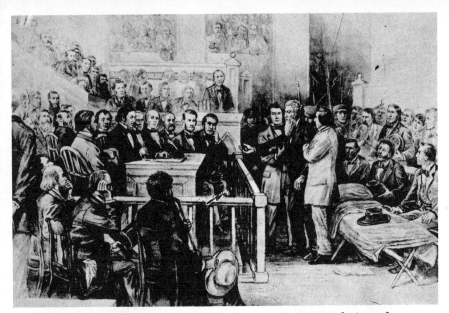

John Brown arraigned for preliminary examination before the eight justices of the peace who formed the Examining Board. (From the New York Public Library Picture Collection. Artist: James E. Taylor.)

The trial of John Brown in the court house at Charlestown, Virginia (now Charles Town, West Virginia). (Harper's Weekly, November 12, 1859. Artist: David H. Strother-Porte Crayon.)

Portrait of John Brown by an unknown artist. Lake Placid Club Library, Lake Placid, New York.

Part V

"Slavery in all its forms will disappear. What the South slew last December was not John Brown, but Slavery. The American Union must be considered dissolved. Between the North and the South stands the gallows of Brown. Union is no longer possible; such a crime cannot be shared."

Victor Hugo, March 30, 1860.

A s soon as it became apparent that John Brown would not die of his wounds, the Commonwealth of Virginia realized that it had an additional problem on its hands. John Brown and the other survivors of the raid would have to be brought to trial.

Immediately, there arose the crucial question of jurisdiction: would Virginia or the Federal Government try John Brown and the other survivors? At that particular juncture of American history, the issue of Federal versus States Rights was being fought and tested. Virginia, in common with other Southern states, was anxious to advance the position of the sovereign power of the states; she elected to try John Brown in her courts. No attempt was made by the Federal Government to take jurisdiction of the case; indeed, the Federal Government conveniently stood aside.

George F. Caskie, in a paper read before the Virginia Bar Association during August, 1909, and subsequently printed and reprinted several times, sums up the issue succinctly:

> When Brown reached Harper's Ferry his first act was to take possession of the United States' property, and to overpower and remove United States guards found there. When finally captured, it was by United States troops upon United States property, after a fight in which one of the United States Marines was killed. Were these occurrences to take place today, it will hardly be doubted that jurisdiction of the whole matter would be taken by the United States courts.

In addition to the South's struggle to gain legal precedence over Federal power, Virginia had another pressing reason for trying John Brown in her courts. If he were to be tried in a Federal Court, the trial would be held over until the spring term. Moreover, in all probability, a change of venue could be obtained on the grounds of prejudice. However, the Virginia statutes of that day read:

> An indictment is found against a person for felony, in a court wherein he may be tried, the accused, if in custody, shall, unless good cause be shown for a continuance, be arraigned and tried in the same term.

The Virginia Grand Jury was in session at that very time; further, the semi-annual term of the Circuit Court was also in session. Thus, "unless good cause for a continuance" were found, John Brown could be arraigned and tried in that same term. A delay would mean holding over his trial until the following April. Virginia had no intention of holding John Brown for another six months; she was determined to try him at once.

Thus it was that on the morning of October 25, 1859, exactly one week after his capture, John Brown and the other four who had been captured were arraigned for preliminary examination. Eight justices of the peace formed the Examining Board.

The examining justices asked John Brown if he had counsel. A few days before the arraignment, John Brown had written identical letters to Judge Daniel R. Tilden of Cleveland, Judge Thomas Russell of Boston, and Reuben A. Chapman of Springfield, Massachusetts, whom he knew from his days in the wool business:

I am here a prisoner with several sabre cuts in my head, and bayonet stabs in my body. My object in writing to you is to obtain able, and faithful counsel for myself; and fellow prisoners as we have the faith of Virginia, pledged through her Governor to give us a fair trial. Without we can obtain such counsel from without the slave states: neither the facts in our case can come before the world: nor can *we* have the benefit of such facts upon our trial. Can you or some other good man come in immediately for the sake of the young men prisoners at least? My wounds are doing well. Do not send an ultra Abolitionist.

Since John Brown's letters had been written only a few days earlier, it was impossible for him to have had a reply. When he was asked by the examining justices (prior to their appointing counsel for him) if he had a lawyer, John Brown uttered the first of several stirring speeches in court. During the interval after his capture, John Brown had used the press to disseminate his word; now, although his speeches were addressed to the business at hand, he was using the courts of the enemy to speak to his countrymen both North and South:

Virginians, I did not ask for any quarter at the time I was taken. I did not ask to have my life spared. The Governor of the State of Virginia tendered me his assurance that I should have a fair trial. If you seek my blood, you can have it at any moment, without this mockery of a trial. I have had no counsel; I have not been able to advise with any one. I am utterly unable to attend in any way to my own defence. My memory don't serve me: my health is insufficient, although improving. If we are to be forced with a mere form—a trial for execution—you might spare yourselves that trouble. I beg for no mockery of a trial— no insult—nothing but that which conscience gives, or cowardice would drive you to practice. I do not even know what the special design of this examination is. I do not know what is to be the benefit of it to the Commonwealth. I have now little further to ask, other than that I may not be foolishly insulted only as cowardly barbarians insult those who fall into their power.

Two able Southern lawyers were appointed to defend John Brown and the machinery of the court moved ahead swiftly. The examining justices unanimously agreed that John Brown and his fellow prisoners were guilty of the offenses charged against them; that same afternoon the case was presented to the Grand Jury.

By noon of the next day, the Grand Jury returned its indictment against the five prisoners. They were accused of treason to the Commonwealth of Virginia; of advising and conspiring with slaves and others to commit treason; of murder in the first degree. Immediately John Brown and the other defendants were ordered from the jail into the courthouse to hear the reading of the arraignment against them. When the jailer went into John Brown's cell to bring him to court, he found John Brown in bed. Refusing to get out of bed and go to the court, John Brown was carried there on a cot. From the cot, he entered a plea for delay:

I do not intend to detain the court, but barely wish to say, as I have been promised a fair trial, that I am not now in circumstances that enable to me to attend a trial, owing to the state of my health. I have a severe wound in the back, or rather in one kidney, which enfeebles me very much. My hearing is impaired and rendered indistinct in consequence of wounds I have about my head. I could not hear what the Court had said this morning. A very short delay would be all I would ask so that I may in some degree recover, and be able at least to listen to my trial, and hear what questions are asked of the citizens, and what their answers are. If that could be allowed to me, I should be very much obliged.

Upon the recommendation of a court physician, Judge Richard Parker refused John Brown's plea for a postponement of the trial. Since each of the prisoners had asked for separate trials, the Commonwealth of Virginia elected to try John Brown first. That same afternoon a jury was selected.

A pool of 38 persons was called from Jefferson County. Out of these, 24 upon being questioned, stated that they had not formed an opinion regarding the guilt or innocence of John Brown which could prevent their arriving at a verdict free of prejudice. Of these 24, eight were peremptorily challenged and the jury was selected by lot from the remaining 16.

It is indeed quite remarkable that out of the first 38 potential jurors called, 24 were found free from prejudice! To assume that the 12 on the jury had not formed an opinion of the case, transcends reality. Certainly it would seem that his counsel should have fought for a change of venue; yet his court-appointed lawyers did not even make such a motion, much less fight for it.

Thus, within 48 hours, Virginia had arraigned the prisoners for preliminary examination, brought them before the Grand Jury, appointed counsel for John Brown and selected a jury for his trial.

The trial proper started the next morning. It lasted three and one-half days. During the middle of the trial, lawyers from the East *did* come to participate, and subsequently took over the case. When they asked for a delay of a few hours in order to acquaint themselves with the indictment and with the criminal code of Virginia, the prosecuting attorney objected. The judge sustained the objection, ordering the trial to proceed at once on the grounds that John Brown had been appointed able counsel; having made the change of lawyers he must bear the consequences.

The North was outraged at this show of unwarranted haste. On November 4, 1859, *The Boston Transcript* said:

> The course pursued at the trial of Old Brown is a disgrace to the civilization of the age. Can anyone read his simple, touching, and yet plucky appeal for delay without a tear? He was exhausted, wounded, partially deaf. Did anyone ever before know a case where a man was on trial for his life, and was denied such a request?

John A. Andrew, eminent attorney and sober citizen of Boston, when examined before the already referred to Congressional Committee on February 9, 1860, accurately reflected the prevalent attitude:

> When the intelligence reached Boston by telegraph that the local court in Jefferson county, Virginia, was proceeding to the trial of John Brown with such speed and hurried action on its part as to render it probable that there was to be no sufficient opportunity to make a full and complete defense, and under such circumstances as that the physical condition of the men themselves seemed to render it entirely improbable that they could prepare a defense with propriety, it struck my mind, and the minds of various other gentlemen whom I met with in the ordinary avocations of my business, in the street, the office, the court rooms, and otherwise, as being a judicial outrage. I certainly felt it to be such. It was wholly unlike anything I had ever known or heard of in my practice as a lawyer.

It is true that John Brown was hurried to trial while still suffering from wounds and without time to prepare his case adequately. It is also true that he had lawyers not of his choosing. But let us suppose that he had not been brought to trial until completely healed, and let us further suppose that he had had counsel of his own choos-

[154]

ing. Would the verdict, ultimately, have been any different?

John Brown could raise the moral issue and say that he dared to break the laws of government—more, that it was men's right and duty to do so in order to exercise a higher loyalty to humanity. In a letter from prison dated November 23, 1859, to Reverend James W. McFarland of Wooster, Ohio, he uttered this thought: "I went against the laws of men, it is true; but 'whether it be right to obey God or men, judge ye.' " Further, he could claim that he should be treated according to the rules of war; as explored earlier, John Brown considered slavery a state of war wherein a powerful majority exercised violence against a defenseless minority.

Thus, John Brown could raise moral issues, but the judge and jury would determine his fate within the framework of the law of the land: a law which justified the institution of slavery. In the eyes of the South, John Brown had invaded a peaceful and quiet town in the middle of the night and had shot down innocent citizens who were defending their hearthstones. Attorney Andrew Hunter, appointed as special prosecutor for Virginia, in his argument dismissed as absurd the claim that John Brown be treated according to the rules of warfare; Hunter contended that John Brown was nothing more than a desperado in command of a gang of murderers.

It is true that Attorney Hunter had to do some tall stretching to accommodate the charge of treason since John Brown was not a citizen of Virginia when he raided Harpers Ferry and owed the state no allegiance. How then could he have committed treason against Virginia? Hunter's contention on this point was:

> The code of Virginia defines citizens of Virginia as "all white persons born in any other State of this Union, who may become residents here;" and that evidence shows without a shadow of a question that when Brown went to Virginia, and planted his feet at Harper's Ferry, he came there

to reside, and to hold the place permanently. True, he occupied a farm four or five miles off in Maryland, but not for the legitimate purpose of establishing his domicile there; no, for the nefarious and hellish purpose of rallying forces into this Commonwealth, and establishing himself at Harper's Ferry, as the starting-point for a new government.

But even if this charge had not been raised, there still remained that basic charge of murder in the first degree. However, in addition to the legal questions, something else was at stake. Time. John Brown needed time in order to continue for as long as possible his battle with the word. Virginia wanted haste; John Brown wanted deliberation. There *was* one way in which John Brown could have escaped hanging—if the issue of insanity were raised, and if then, upon examination, he were found to be insane. This issue *was* raised by his Southern counsel when they received a wire dated October 27, from A. H. Lewis, editor of the *Summit Beacon*, Akron, Ohio:

> John Brown, leader of the insurrection at Harper's Ferry, and several of his family, have resided in this county many years. Insanity is hereditary in that family. His mother's sister died with it, and a daughter of that sister has been two years in a lunatic asylum. A son and daughter of his mother's brother have also been confined in the lunatic asylum, and another son of that brother is now insane and under close restraint. These facts can be conclusively proven by witnesses residing here, who will doubtless attend the trial if desired.

Subsequent to the trial, in an attempt to gain clemency, 19 affidavits were gathered from friends and relatives in Ohio further attesting to the fact that there was insanity on John Brown's mother's side. Louis Ruchames, in his *A John Brown Reader*, puts the situation well regarding these affidavits:

> Putting aside the basic question of whether one's insanity

may be established by the presence or absence of insanity in one's family, it may be noted that the affidavits are highly suspect as valid evidence. Their primary purpose was to save Brown from execution by showing him to be insane. They must, therefore, be regarded not as objective reports but as partisan statements made to achieve a certain purpose, with every possibility that the material they present may be biased in the direction of proving insanity. Moreover, their reliability as evidence is weakened still further by the fact that they include significant sections which are based, quite explicitly, not on direct knowledge but on hearsay and secondhand information.

Many of the affidavits do not stand up under investigation, though there can be little doubt that there was insanity on the mother's side of the family. The legal determination for sanity, namely a mental examination, was never pursued. For a brief time it seemed that John Brown would have such an examination, for Governor Wise wrote an instruction for Dr. Francis T. Stribling, Superintendent of the Lunatic Asylum of Staunton, Virginia, to come to Charlestown and examine the defendant:

If the prisoner is insane he ought to be cured, and if not insane the fact ought to be vouched in the most reliable form, now that it is questioned under oath and by counsel since conviction.

Unfortunately, the unpredictable Governor Wise changed his mind and the instruction was never sent to Dr. Stribling. As for Governor Wise's own opinion on the matter, he was earlier quoted when the attack on Harpers Ferry was ascribed to be the act of a madman: "And they are themselves mistaken who take him to be a madman." Subsequently, after further interviews with John Brown, Governor Wise addressed the Virginia Legislature and said:

I know that he was sane and remarkably sane, if quick and

clear perception, if assumed rational premises and consecutive reasoning from them, if cautious tact in avoiding disclosures and in covering conclusions and inferences, if memory and conception and practical common sense, and if composure and self-possession are evidence of a sound state of mind.

In court, when John Brown's Southern counsel introduced the Ohio affidavits, John Brown raised himself from his cot and said:

I look upon it as a miserable artifice and pretext of those who ought to take a different course in regard to me, and I view it with contempt more than otherwise. Insane persons, so far as my experience goes, have but little ability to judge of their own sanity; and if I am insane, of course I should think I know more than all the rest of the world. But I do not think so. I am perfectly unconscious of insanity, and I reject, so far as I am capable, any attempt to interfere in my behalf on that score.

John Brown well understood that if the raid on Harpers Ferry could be ascribed to the act of a madman, the meaning of his life would be destroyed. He had risked his life for his cause for many years; he had no intention at this juncture of trying to save it at the expense of his cause. He refused to allow his counsel to enter a plea of insanity.

During the afternoon of Monday, October 31, 1859, the fourth day of the trial, the jury withdrew to consider the evidence. After 45 minutes of deliberation the jury returned with a unanimous verdict of guilty on all three counts: conspiring with slaves to rebel; treason; murder.

During the next two days John Brown's counsel made a motion for arrest of judgment; there was argument on the motion, and Judge Parker rendered his opinion wherein he stated his reasons for overruling the objections made regarding the judgment. On November 2, John Brown was brought from jail into the courtroom and was asked if he had anything to say before sentence was pronounced. He had not expected to receive sentence until after the trial of the other defendants and was therefore unprepared. However, he began, as has been described, to speak "with perfect calmness of voice and mildness of manner." This speech, although not taught in the schools, is an American prose epic. When Ralph Waldo Emerson delivered a funeral address for Abraham Lincoln, he compared John Brown's address to the court with Lincoln's at Gettysburg. Said Emerson:

> His brief speech at Gettysburg will not easily be surpassed by words on any recorded occasion. This and one other American speech, that of John Brown to the court that tried him, and a part of Kossuth's speech at Birmingham, can only be compared with each other, and with no fourth.

Here, in part, is John Brown's address which he delivered to the court—and to the nation as well:

> Had I interfered in the manner which I admit, had I so interfered in behalf of the rich, the powerful, the intelligent, the so-called great, or in behalf of any of their friends, either father, mother, brother, sister, wife or children, or any of that class, and suffered and sacrificed what I have in this interference, it would have been all right. Every man in this court would have deemed it an act worthy of reward rather than punishment.
>
> This court acknowledges too, as I suppose, the validity of the law of God. I see a book kissed, which I suppose to be the Bible, or at least the New Testament, which teaches me that all things whatsoever I would that men should do to me, I should do even so to them. I endeavored to act up to that instruction. I say I am yet too young to understand that God is any respecter of persons. I believe that to have interfered as I have done, as I always have freely admitted I have done, in behalf of His despised poor, I did not wrong, but right. Now, if it is deemed necessary that I should forfeit my life for the furtherance of the ends of justice, and mingle my blood further with the blood of my children

and with the blood of millions in this slave country whose rights are disregarded by wicked, cruel and unjust enactments, I submit. So let it be done.

The two prongs of his God-driven ethical consciousness are here once again enunciated and linked together: the Golden Rule, and man's duty to intercede in behalf of the millions of slaves whose rights have been violated by unjust laws. But in addition to this, he enunciates with great clarity a strong class position in the matter of slavery, placing the rich and powerful against the despised poor.

When John Brown concluded, the judge, in a quiet voice, pronounced sentence. The prisoner was to be hanged in a public place on December 2, 1859.

If John Brown was to achieve his victory, he had 30 days more to do so.

*　　*　　*　　*　　*　　*

When Frederick Douglass delivered his address on John Brown at Storer College, he said, "When John Brown stretched forth his arm the sky was cleared. The time for compromises was gone, the clash of arms was at hand." That the raid on Harpers Ferry was the catalyst forcing the issue of war, was well understood by both sides. On October 21, three days after John Brown's capture, the *Richmond Enquirer* editorialized:

The "Irrepressible Conflict" was initiated at Harper's Ferry, and though there, for the time suppressed, yet no man is able to say when or where it will begin again or where it will end. Is there no remedy? Shall the South, divided by useless conflicts about Federal politics, fall as single victims to marauding bands of Northern fanatics? Can there be no union of council, actions and *arms* among States so vitally interested in the integrity of each?

Four days later it answered its own questions:

[160]

The Harper's Ferry invasion has advanced the cause of Disunion more than any other event that has happened since the formation of the Government; it has revived with tenfold strength the desires of a Southern Confederacy. The, heretofore, most determined friends of the Union may now be heard saying, "If our peace is disturbed, our States invaded, its peaceful citizens cruelly murdered, *and the people of the North sustain the outrage*, then let disunion come."

In the North, Horace Greeley wrote that the raid "presses on the 'irrepressible conflict,' and I think the end of slavery in Virginia and the Union is ten years nearer than it seemed a few weeks ago." Thus, (and again the irony) while John Brown's raid had served notice to both sides that arms would soon replace words, John Brown, divested of his sword and in prison, well understood that from this moment on, the word was *his* only weapon.

It was the practice at that time to allow prisoners to have visiting privileges almost without limit. There was a constant stream of visitors to John Brown's cell. On occasion, traffic was so heavy that Captain John Avis, his jailer, had to break up into small groups the large numbers of waiting people. Some of these visitors came out of curiosity to see what manner of man this was, many came with hate. With all who came, John Brown debated and proselytized ceaselessly.

We get a picture of this man at his work through his correspondence. On November 1, in answer to a letter from a Quaker lady in Rhode Island, he writes, "I wish you could know with what cheerfulness I am now wielding the 'sword of the Spirit' on the right hand and on the left. I bless God that it proves 'mighty to the pulling down of strongholds.'" On November 15, answering Reverend H. L. Vaill, who more than 40 years earlier was his teacher at the Morris Academy when he was preparing for the ministry, John Brown writes:

[161]

I have not only been (though utterly unworthy) permitted to suffer affliction with God's people, but have also had a great many rare opportunities for "preaching righteousness in the great congregation." I trust it will not all be lost.

On the 24th, answering a letter from a friend, he writes:

I have very many interesting visits from proslavery persons almost daily, and I endeavor to improve them faithfully, plainly, and kindly. I do not think that I enjoyed life better than since my confinement here.

And, indeed, John Brown must have had a grim, quiet pleasure as he endeavored "faithfully, plainly, and kindly" to improve his visitors.

But he was not "kindly" to gentlemen of the cloth who came offering to pray with him, and, perhaps, to labor with him for his sins. He said to one Southern clergyman, "I will thank you to leave me alone; your prayers would be an abomination to my God." To another he said, "I would not insult God by bowing down in prayer with any-one who had the blood of a slave on his skirts." And to a third who argued in favor of slavery as "a Christian institution," John Brown replied impatiently:

My dear sir, you know nothing about Christianity; you will have to learn its A, B, C; I find you quite ignorant of what the word Christianity means. I respect you as a gentleman, of course, but it is as a heathen gentleman.

And on November 23, in the already quoted letter to Reverend McFarland of Wooster, Ohio, he wrote:

I would be glad to have you, or any of my liberty-loving ministerial friends here, to talk and pray with me. It would be a great pleasure to me to have some one better qualified than myself to lead my mind in prayer and meditation, now that my time is so near a close. You may wonder, are there no ministers of the gospel here? I answer, *No*.

[162]

There are no ministers of *Christ* here. These ministers who profess to be Christian and hold slaves or advocate slavery, I cannot abide them. My knees will not bend in prayer with them while their hands are stained with the blood of souls.

Through that final month of his life, John Brown steadfastly refused to entertain the question of prayer with a Southern clergyman, and on the morning of the hanging, he refused the presence of a minister either in his cell or at the gallows.

It was his letters from prison, especially those to his family, copied and recopied and published in the press, which helped move the attack on Harpers Ferry from the arena of a fanatic to the area of a man who, to quote Thoreau, "did not value his bodily life in comparison with ideal things. He did not recognize unjust human laws, but resisted them as he was bid. For once we are lifted out of the trivialness and dust of politics into the region of truth and manhood."

Southerners raged when Judge Parker pronouncing sentence gave 30 days more of life to John Brown. They would have preferred to cut off at once the torrent of letters which flowed from John Brown's cell to family, friends and the many strangers who wrote to him. It was difficult to stand up against the sentiment and tone of these letters. On October 31, even before sentence was passed on him, in a letter addressed to "My dear Wife, and Children, every one," he writes:

Under all these terrible calamities; I feel quite cheerful in the assurance that God reigns; and will overrule all for his glory; and the best possible good. "These *light* afflictions which are *but for a moment* shall work out for us a far *more exceeding and eternal* weight of glory."

And on November 8, again addressing his letter to "Dear Wife and Children, every one," he writes:

I can trust God with both the time and the manner of my

death, believing, as I now do, that for me at this time to seal my testimony for God and humanity with blood will do vastly more toward advancing the cause I have earnestly endeavored to promote, than all I have done in my life before. Think, too, of the crushed millions who "have no comforter." I charge you all never in your trials to forget the griefs "of the poor that cry, and of those that have none to help them."

And on the 12th he writes to his "Dear Brother Jeremiah:" "I am quite cheerful in view of my approaching end,—being fully persuaded that I am worth inconceivably more to hang than for any other purpose."

And then, addressed to "Dear Children all," he writes on the 22nd:

When and in what form death may come is but of small moment. I feel just as content to die for God's eternal truth and for suffering humanity on the scaffold as in any other way. I now feel it most grateful that I am counted in the least possible degree worthy to suffer for the truth.

And on November 28 he writes to Judge Daniel R. Tilden:

It is a great comfort to feel assured that I am permitted to die (for a cause) not merely to pay the debt of nature, (as all must). I feel myself to be most unworthy of so great distinction. The particular manner of dying assigned to me, gives me but very little uneasiness. I wish I had the time and the ability to give you (my dear friend) some little idea of what is daily, and I might almost say, hourly passing within my prison walls; and could my friends but witness only a few of those scenes just as they occur, I think they would feel very well reconciled to my being here just what I am, and just as I am. My whole life before had not afforded me one half the opportunity to plead for the right.

And on November 30, a few days before he was to be hanged, he writes in a letter addressed to "My Dearly beloved Wife, sons: and Daughters, every one":

[164]

I am waiting the hour of my public murder with great composure of mind, and cheerfulness, feeling the strongest assurance that in no other possible way could I be used to so much advance the cause of God, and of humanity, and that nothing that either I or all my family have sacrificed or suffered will be lost. I have now no doubt that our seeming disaster will ultimately result in the most glorious success. So my dear shattered and broken family, be of good cheer. It is ground of the utmost comfort to my mind to know that so many of you as have had the opportunity have given full proof of your fidelity to the great family of man. Be faithful unto death.

John Brown had other concerns as well—family and farm. On November 21, less than two weeks before he was to hang, he writes to Mary, perhaps a bit plaintively:

Why will you not say to me whether you had any crops mature this season? If so, what ones? Although I may nevermore interfere with your worldy affairs, I have not yet lost all interest in them. A little history of your success or of your failures I should very much prize.

Some of his letters had enormous dramatic impact. Readers were shaken. Mrs. Lydia Maria Child, a Quaker, wrote to Governor Wise asking permission to come to Charlestown and tend John Brown. She also wrote to John Brown volunteering her services. To her letter, John Brown replied on November 4:

Your most kind letter has reached me, with the kind offer to come here and take care of me. Allow me to express my gratitude for your great sympathy, and at the same time to propose to you a different course, together with my reasons for wishing it. First I am so far recovered from my wounds as no longer to require nursing. Then, again, it would subject you to great personal inconvenience and heavy expense, without doing me any good. Allow me to name to you another channel through which you may reach me with your sympathies much more effectively. I have at home a

[165]

wife and three young daughters, the youngest but little over
five years old, the oldest nearly sixteen. I have also two
daughters-in-law, whose husbands have both fallen near
me here. There is also another widow, Mrs. Thompson,
whose husband fell here. I have a middle-aged son who was
a most dreadful sufferer in Kansas, and lost all he had laid
up. He has not enough to clothe himself for the winter com-
fortably. I have no living son or son-in-law who did not
suffer terribly in Kansas.

Now, dear friend, would you not as soon contribute fifty
cents now, and a like sum yearly, for the relief of those very
poor and deeply afflicted persons, to enable them to supply
themselves and their children with bread and very plain
clothing, and to enable the children to receive a common
English education? Will you also devote your own energies
to induce others to join you in giving a like amount, to constitute a little fund for the purpose named?

I cannot see how your coming here can do me the least good;
and I am quite certain you can do me immense good where
you are. God Almighty bless and reward you a thousand-
fold!

Yours in sincerity and truth,

Other persons also wrote letters. John Copeland, Jr., 25,
a free Negro of Oberlin, Ohio, who had been studying in
the preparatory department of Oberlin College at the time
he joined John Brown, was sentenced to be hanged on
December 16. Writing to his brother on December 10,
eight days after the hanging of John Brown and six days
before his own death, he said:

I am not terrified by the gallows upon which I am soon to
stand and suffer death for doing what George Washington
was made a hero for doing, while, for having lent my aid
to a general no less brave, and engaged in a cause no less
honorable and glorious, I am to suffer death. Washington
entered the field to fight for the freedom of the American
people—not for the white man alone, but for both black and

white. Nor were they white men alone who fought for the freedom of this country. The blood of black men flowed as freely as that of white men. Dear brother, could I die in a more noble cause? Could I die in a manner and for a cause which would induce true and honest men more to honor me, and the angels more ready to receive me to their happy home of everlasting joy above?

Hours before he was to be hanged along with John Cook, Shields Green and Edwin Coppoc, he wrote:

Dear Father, Mother, Brothers Henry, William and Freddy, and Sisters Sarah and Mary:

I fully believe that not only myself, but also all three of my poor comrades who are to ascend the same scaffold— (a scaffold already made sacred to the cause of freedom by the death of that great champion of human freedom— Captain John Brown) are *prepared* to meet our God. Dear parents, brothers and sisters, I pray daily and hourly that though we meet no more on earth, we shall meet in heaven, where we shall not be parted by the demands of the cruel and unjust monster Slavery.

In addition to John Brown's letters, there was a great literary outpouring. I have mentioned Thoreau, Parker and Emerson—Emerson who in an address in Boston during November said that John Brown's hanging "will make the gallows as glorious as the Cross." There were also poems by Walt Whitman, Herman Melville, William Dean Howells, Louisa May Alcott, John Greenleaf Whittier, Bronson Alcott, and others. There were articles in the press; speeches were given in town halls. Hundreds of sermons were delivered from Sunday pulpits by the foremost ministers of the day. Many of these sermons were subsequently printed in pamphlet form. Sold in thousands, they found their way into many homes where they were avidly read. Even across the Atlantic, John Brown and his raid engendered heated partisanship. Victor Hugo, in exile at that time on the Isle of Guernsey, wrote a letter to the editor of the *London News* wherein he made the prediction:

Politically speaking, the murder of Brown would be an irrevocable mistake. It would penetrate the Union with a secret fissure, which would in the end tear it asunder. It is possible that the execution of Brown might consolidate Slavery in Virginia, but it is certain that it would convulse the entire American Democracy. You preserve your shame, but you sacrifice your glory.

And on March 30, 1860, Hugo wrote:

Slavery in all its forms will disappear. What the South slew last December was not John Brown, but Slavery. The American Union must be considered dissolved. Between the North and the South stands the gallows of Brown. Union is no longer possible: such a crime cannot be shared.

The 30 days passed; the span of life allotted to John Brown by Judge Parker had come to an end. Two weeks before, John Brown had written to Reverend H. L. Vaill:

As I believe most firmly that God reigns; I cannot believe that anything I have done suffered or may yet suffer will be lost; to the cause of God or of humanity: and before I began my work at Harpers Ferry; I felt assured that in the worst *event;* it would certainly PAY. I often expressed that belief; and I can now see no possible cause to alter my mind.

It was this knowledge that he *had* won his battle that gave him serenity and patience; he was even gravely triumphant. During his stay in prison many plans were drawn up for his escape. Some were wildly unfeasible; but others, though daring, had possible chances of success. To all of these plans, when word deviously was brought to John Brown, he turned a deaf ear. In his prison letters

[168]

we find statements such as: "I think I cannot now better serve the cause I love so much than to die for it; and in my death I may do more than in my life." And again, "I think that perhaps my object would be nearer fulfillment if I should die." And still again, "For me at this time to seal my testimony for God and humanity with my blood will do vastly more toward advancing the cause I have earnestly endeavored to promote, than all I have done in my life before." Virginia needed no prison, no shackles around his ankles, no jailer to guard him, for when John Brown said that he "would not walk out of the prison if the door was left open," he meant exactly that. He knew that he must die to achieve his objective, and he intended to achieve it.

On the morning of December 2, in Cambridge, Massachusetts, Henry Wadsworth Longfellow wrote in his journal:

This will be a great day in our history; the date of a new Revolution,—quite as much needed as the old one. Even now as I write, they are leading Old John Brown to execution in Virginia for attempting to rescue slaves! This is sowing the wind to reap the whirlwind, which will come soon.

Sheriff James W. Campbell and Captain Avis entered the cell and bound John Brown's hands behind him. Then they led him through the door and toward a waiting carriage drawn by two large horses, well matched as to size and style. The bed of the carriage contained only an empty coffin. Earlier that morning John Brown had written a message to his countrymen which he now gave to Hiram O'Bannon, a guard at the jail:

I, John Brown am now quite certain that the crimes of this guilty land: will never be purged away; but with Blood. I had as I now think: vainly flattered myself that without very much bloodshed; it might be done.

[169]

The Puritan speaks in that first sentence. The nation is guilty of a great crime perpetrated on a portion of its people; it is also guilty before God for transforming men and women with divine souls into property. For this crime to God and man, there is no remission of sin except through the purge of blood. But it is the second sentence of this two-sentence legacy which always saddens me, for I read in it the sadness which I think John Brown must have felt when he wrote it. For here John Brown refers to his plan for the move into the wilderness of the Allegheny Mountains. We know from history that victory is infinitely less costly when achieved by guerrilla fighting than the confrontation of hundreds of thousands of soldiers in massed conventional warfare. John Brown envisaged his guerrilla fighting in the mountains as a means of weakening the institution of slavery and ultimately toppling it. But now that his plans were destroyed, the nation was doomed to blood and flames.

When John Brown emerged from the jail and looked about him, he exclaimed sardonically, "I had no idea that Governor Wise considered my execution so important." Three companies of infantry, fully armed and with bayonets fixed, were stationed ahead of the wagon. To the rear and on both sides, other companies were positioned. Cavalrymen and more clusters of infantry were stationed at strategic points along the way. At the site of the gallows, as far as the eye could see, armed soldiers to the number of 1,500, were on duty. There were also cannon. Stretching out in an ever-thinning perimeter several miles away, were an additional 1,500 soldiers guarding the roads and other points of access.

Since his hands were bound, John Brown could not mount the carriage unaided. Sheriff Campbell and Captain Avis helped him over the tailgate and indicated that he was to seat himself on the empty coffin. The carriage started on its journey to the scaffold situated in an open field about a mile away.

Mary Brown arriving at Charlestown, Virginia, on December 1, 1859, to pay a last visit to her husband the night before his hanging. (Frank Leslie's Illustrated Paper, *December 17, 1859. Artist: Alfred Berghaus.*)

John and Mary Brown at their last meal together in the parlor of Captain John Avis, jailer. (New York Illustrated News, *December 17, 1859. Artist: D. C. Hitchcock.*)

Captain John Avis, jailer of John Brown. (Collection of Boyd B. Stutler.)

Charlestown, Va, 2ᵈ December, 1859.

John Brown am now quite <u>certain</u> that the crimes of this guilty, <u>land</u>: <u>will</u> never be purged away; but with Blood: I had <u>as I now</u> think: <u>vainly</u> flattered myself that without <u>very much bloodshed</u>; it might be done.

John Brown's last statement. This message to his countrymen was given to Hiram O'Bannon, a guard at the jail, on the morning of the hanging.

John Brown, bound and seated on his coffin, riding to the gallows, December 2, 1859. (Frank Leslie's Illustrated Paper, December 17, 1859.)

The procession from the jail to the scaffold. (New York Illustrated News, *December 17, 1859. Artist: David C. Hitchcock.*)

John Brown ascending the scaffold. (Frank Leslie's Illustrated Paper, *December 17, 1859.*)

The hanging of John Brown. This sketch was drawn by David H. Strother (Porte Crayon) for Harper's Weekly *but not used at that time. (Collection of Boyd B. Stutler.)*

John Brown's grave at his farm in North Elba, New York.

It was a beautifully clear day, warm and sunny, and the sky was bright blue. As the wagon reached the open field where the scaffold was erected, John Brown, hands bound and seated on his coffin, looked out over the field toward the mountains which he had hoped were to be his refuge and strength, and said, "This *is* a beautiful country. I never had the pleasure of seeing it before."

John Brown ascended the steps of the scaffold. The hood was placed over his head and the noose around his neck. He was led to the trap door and placed over it. The troops below were to be formed into two hollow squares, one within the other. Whether because of inexperience or by design, it took 12 minutes of marching manoeuver to get the troops in position, during which time John Brown stood on the trap door, waiting. At last the word was given and the trap door sprung.

> Year of meteors! brooding years!
> I would bind in words retrospective some of your deeds and
>   signs, . . .
> I would sing how an old man, tall, with white hair, mounted
>   the scaffold in Virginia,
> (I was at hand, silent I stood with teeth shut close, I watch'd,
> I stood very near you old man when cool and indifferent, but
>   trembling with age and your unheal'd wounds,
>   you mounted the scaffold:)

So wrote Walt Whitman in his poem, *Year of Meteors (1859-60)*, describing his feelings when, in imagination, he was present at the hanging. There was another man who actually *was* there who would not at all subscribe to the feelings Walt Whitman expressed. This other man, 21 years old and an actor, had joined the Virginia militia and had been assigned to Company F in Richmond. Along with many other militia companies of Virginia brought in from the surrounding cities, Company F was present that morning. The young actor-soldier was a member of the inside hollow square and watched the proceedings with great interest. His name was John Wilkes Booth; six years later at Ford's Theatre in Washington he assassinated Abraham Lincoln.

During the first days of John Brown's imprisonment, he pleaded with Mary not to come to visit him. In his letter of November 8, addressed to "Dear Wife and Children, Every one," writing to Mary in the third person, he explains his reasons:

First, it would use up all the scanty means she has, or is at all likely to have, to make herself and children comfortable hereafter. For let me tell you that the sympathy that is now aroused in your behalf may not always follow you. There is but little more of the Romantic about helping poor widows and their children than there is about trying to relieve poor "niggers." Again, the little comfort it might afford us to meet again would be dearly bought by the pains of a final separation. We must part; and I feel assured for us to meet under such dreadful circumstances would only add to our distress. If she comes on here, she must be only a gazing-stock throughout the whole journey, to be remarked upon in every look, word, and action, and by all sorts of creatures, and by all sorts of papers, throughout the whole country. Oh, Mary! do not come, but patiently wait for the meeting of those who love God and their fellow-men, where no separation must follow. "They shall go no more out forever."

A week later, on the 16th, in a letter addressed to "My Dear Wife," his resolve begins to falter:

If you feel sure that you can endure the trials and the shock which will be unavoidable (if you come), I should be most glad to see you once more; but when I think of your being insulted on the road, and perhaps while here, I shrink from it. If you do come, defer your journey till about the 27th or 28th of this month. The scenes which you will have to pass

[172]

through will be anything but those you now pass, with tender, kind-hearted friends, and kind faces to meet you everywhere. Do consider the matter well before you make the plunge.

By the 26th, he writes Mary: "If you now feel that you are equal to the undertaking, do exactly as you feel disposed to do about coming to see me suffer. I am entirely· willing."

In this same letter, discussing the disposal of his body and that of his two sons, Oliver and Watson, he says:

> I am inclined to think you will not be likely to succeed well about getting away the bodies of your family; but should that be so: Do not let that grieve you. It can make but little difference what is done with them.

Nevertheless, Mary Brown wrote to Governor Wise and obtained permission from him to receive the mortal remains of her husband. The day before the hanging, she had arrived by train in Harpers Ferry; escorted by a troop of soldiers, she took the long carriage ride to Charlestown. There she spent the hours of the late afternoon and early evening with her husband and was then escorted by the soldiers back to the hotel in Harpers Ferry. She waited in the hotel as instructed until the next day when the coffin containing the body was to be delivered to her.

Preparations were immediately made to transport the body to the farm in North Elba, high in the Adirondack Mountains of New York, for burial. As the train bearing his body moved East and then North, solemn church bells rang out. The bells rang in Ravenna, in Cleveland, in Philadelphia, in New York, in Rochester, in Syracuse, in Vergennes, in Fitchburg, in Plymouth, in Concord, Massachusetts, and in Concord, New Hampshire, in New Bedford, in Manchester, in Providence, in Albany, in Troy, in Rutland, and in Westport. The funeral cortege stayed overnight at Elizabethtown, New York; the coffin was

[173]

reverently placed in the courthouse, and a guard of honor was stationed through the night.

He was buried on December 8, 1859. He had asked to be buried in the shadow of a great granite rock, and he was so buried. His body in the shadow of the great granite rock; the granite rock in the shadow of the great granite White Mountain which he loved so dear. The granite thrust of his will, the granite thrust of his Old Testament conscience, the granite of the mountains, all were now one.

From this tiny village, North Elba, situated high in the Adirondack Mountains, six men were lost in the raid on Harpers Ferry; two were the sons of John and Mary Brown. All six were intertwined into one family, relatives either by blood or by marriage. The women of these inter-twined families suffered grievous loss. They stood around the open grave of John Brown and listened to Wendell Phillips, orator and abolitionist:

He has abolished slavery in Virginia. History will date Virginia Emancipation from Harper's Ferry. True, the slave is still there. So, when the tempest uproots a pine on your hills, it looks green for months,—a year or two. Still, it is timber, not a tree. John Brown has loosened the roots of the slave system; it only breathes,—it does not live,—hereafter.

Seventeen months after the hanging of John Brown, the first shots were fired at Fort Sumter, ushering in the Civil War. John Brown's apocalyptic statement the morning of his hanging, "I, John Brown, am now quite certain that the crimes of this guilty land will never be purged away but with blood," had become a tragic reality.

BIBLIOGRAPHY

The following are the books, speeches, reports and documents which have been most useful:

American Anti-Slavery Society Twenty-Seventh Annual Report. *The Anti-Slavery History of the John Brown Year.* New York: American Anti-Slavery Society, 1861.

Aptheker, Herbert, (ed. and with commentary). *A Documentary History of the Negro People in the United States.* New York: The Citadel Press, 1951.

Benét, Stephen Vincent, *John Brown's Body.* New York: Rinehart and Co., Inc., 1928.

Buckmaster, Henrietta, *Let My People Go.* New York: Harper and Brothers, 1941.

Douglass, Frederick, *Narrative of the Life of Frederick Douglass.* Boston: Anti-Slavery Society, 1845.

———, *My Bondage and My Freedom.* New York and Auburn: Miller, Orton and Mulligan, 1855.

———, *The Life and Times of Frederick Douglass.* Hartford: Park Publishing Company, 1881.

DuBois, W. E. B., *John Brown.* Philadelphia: George W. Jacobs and Co., 1909.

Ehrlich, Leonard, *God's Angry Man.* New York: Simon and Schuster, Inc., 1932.

Foner, Philip S., (ed.) *The Life and Writings of Frederick Douglass.* Four Volumes (See especially Vol. II). Also contains a biography of Douglass by the editor. New York: International Publishers Co., Inc., 1950.

Helper, Hinton Rowan, *The Impending Crisis of the South: How To Meet It.* New York: A. B. Burdick, 1860.

Hendrick, Burton J., *Statesmen of the Lost Cause.* Boston: Little, Brown and Co., 1939.

Higginson, Thomas Wentworth, *Cheerful Yesterdays.* Boston: Houghton, Mifflin and Co., 1898.

———, *Contemporaries.* (See especially the chapter, "A Visit to John Brown's Household in 1859.") Boston: Houghton, Mifflin and Co., 1899.

———, *Army Life in a Black Regiment* (with an introduction by Howard N. Meyer). New York: Collier Books, 1962.

Hinton Richard J., *John Brown and His Men: With Some Account of the Roads They Travelled to Reach Harper's Ferry.* New York: Funk and Wagnalls Co., 1894.

Hofstadter, Richard, *The American Political Tradition and the Men Who Made It.* New York: Alfred A. Knopf, Inc., 1948. (See the chapters on John C. Calhoun, Abraham Lincoln and Wendell Phillips.)

Karsner, David, *John Brown of Harper's Ferry.* New York: Dodd, Mead and Co., 1934.

Lonn, Ella, *Desertion During the Civil War.* New York: The Century Co., 1928.

The Mason Report. The report of the Select Committee of the Senate appointed to inquire into the late invasion and seizure of the public property at Harper's Ferry; Rep. Com. No. 278. 36th Congress, 1st Session. (Generally known as *The Mason Report* after Senator James M. Mason of Virginia who headed the investigation.)

Meyer, Howard N., *Colonel of the Black Regiment: The Life of Thomas Wentworth Higginson.* New York: W. W. Norton and Co., Inc., 1967.

Miller, Ernest C., *John Brown: Pennsylvania Citizen.* Warren, Pennsylvania: The Penn State Press, 1952. (A pamphlet dealing with John Brown's ten years in Pennsylvania.)

Moore, Albert Burton, *Conscription and Conflict in the Confederacy,* New York: Hillary House, 1924.

Nelson, Truman, *The Surveyor*. New York: Doubleday and Co., Inc., 1960.

Newton, John, *Captain John Brown of Harper's Ferry*. New York: A. Wessels Co., 1902.

Owsley, Frank Lawrence, *King Cotton Diplomacy*. Chicago: University of Chicago Press, 1931.

Quarles, Benjamin, *The Negro in the Civil War*. Boston: Little, Brown and Co., 1953.

Redpath, James, *The Public Life of Captain John Brown*. Boston: Thayer and Eldridge, 1860.

Ruchames, Louis, (ed. and with commentary) *A John Brown Reader*. New York: Abelard-Schuman, 1959.

Sanborn, Franklin Benjamin, *The Life and Letters of John Brown*. Boston: Roberts Brothers, 1891.

———, *Recollections of Seventy Years*. Two Volumes. Boston: The Gorham Press, 1909.

Stampp, Kenneth M., (ed. and with commentary) *The Causes of the Civil War*. Englewood Cliffs, New Jersey: Prentice-Hall, Inc., 1959.

Tatum, Georgia Lee, *Disloyalty in the Confederacy*. Chapel Hill: University of North Carolina Press, 1934.

Thoreau, Henry David, *A Plea for Captain John Brown*. Address delivered on October 30, 1859.

———, *After the Death of John Brown*. Address delixered on December 2, 1859.

———, *The Last Days of John Brown*. Address delivered on July 4, 1860.

———, *The Writings of Henry David Thoreau*. Boston: Houghton, Mifflin and Co., 1893. (Vol. 10 contains all three speeches cited above.)

Villard, Oswald Garrison, *John Brown, 1800–1859: A Biography Fifty Years After*. Boston: Houghton Mifflin Co., 1910. (Revised and reprinted in 1943 by Alfred A. Knopf, Inc.)

Von Holst, Hermann, *John Brown*. Boston: Cupples and Hurd, 1889.

The reader interested in additional source material is referred to the excellent bibliography to be found in *John Brown, 1800–1859: A Biography Fifty Years After*. This list proved invaluable.

*   *   *   *   *   *

For the convenience of those interested in specific aspects of this book, the following may be helpful:

1. JOHN BROWN'S LIFE:
   The Public Life of John Brown by James Redpath. The first biography of John Brown. Redpath knew him personally. His book was published soon after the hanging and has an intense immediacy.

   John Brown and His Men by Richard J. Hinton. Hinton was to have joined John Brown in the raid on Harpers Ferry. Enroute, he learned that the raid had already begun and turned back. His book is replete with invaluable material. In addition, there is an excellent appendix "Containing the principal and more important documents prepared by John Brown, or relating directly to the enterprises against American slavery in which he was actually engaged."

   The Life and Letters of John Brown by Franklin Benjamin Sanborn. Sanborn was one of the "Secret Six," and had intimate knowledge of their undercover planning with John Brown. Contains a splendid collection of letters of John Brown and others connected with him.

   John Brown by W. E. B. DuBois. This biography by one of the greatest black scholars has formidable insights about John Brown. The section dealing with John Brown's plans to conduct guerrilla operations in the Alleghenies after the raid is particularly perceptive.

   John Brown, 1800–1859: A Biography Fifty Years After by Oswald Garrison Villard. A most extensively researched work; enormously valuable, with particularly good material on Kansas. However, Villard distorts the essence and meaning of the Chatham Convention, and is mistaken

[178]

regarding John Brown's basic strategy for the attack on Harper's Ferry.

2. FREDERICK DOUGLASS:
Narrative of the Life of Frederick Douglass; My Bondage and My Freedom; The Life and Times of Frederick Douglass; all by Frederick Douglass. Three major autobiographical works by a central figure of 19th Century America. A view of the world by an escaped slave who became one of the great leaders of his people.
The Life and Writings of Frederick Douglass. These four volumes have been edited by Philip S. Foner. In addition, there is a biography of Douglass by the editor. Douglass's brilliant mind covered the full range of the period. Volume II, covering the pre-Civil war decade of 1850–60, is of particular interest to those concerned with John Brown.

3. THE NEGRO IN AMERICA and THE ABOLITION MOVEMENT:
A Documentary History of the Negro People in the United States, edited and with commentary by Herbert Aptheker. Beginning with the pre-Revolutionary era and continuing into the 20th Century, Aptheker traces the history of the Negro in America through a unique collection of documents written only by blacks. These documents include letters, pamphlets, protests, proposals and programs, political discussions, social manifestos, petitions and heart-rending personal statements. Aptheker's introductory notes and skill in organizing the material make this a truly fascinating volume. Essential for anyone who seeks an understanding of black history.
Let My People Go by Henrietta Buckmaster. The author has sub-titled this work, "The Story of the Underground Railroad and the Growth of the Abolition Movement." It is a magnificent study of these two topics individually and as they relate to each other. Passionately and beautifully written. Available in paperback.

[179]

Army Life in a Black Regiment by Thomas Wentworth Higginson. During 1862, Thomas Wentworth Higginson took command of the just formed First South Carolina Volunteers. This regiment consisted of newly freed, runaway slaves; it was the first black regiment so formed. Colonel Higginson and his men knew that if captured by Confederate forces they would not be treated as prisoners of war; they would be summarily hanged. Higginson kept a diary of his experiences as commanding officer of this black regiment. A superb and important book, recently reprinted in paperback with an excellent introduction by Howard N. Meyer.

The Negro in the Civil War by Benjamin Quarles. After the Civil War, Secretary of War Stanton stated: "The whole contest would have gone against us if we had not got 200,000 negroes to come and join our armies and turn the tide of victory on our side." This fine book details the significant contribution of the blacks to the winning of the Civil War.

4. ECONOMY OF THE SOUTH:

King Cotton Diplomacy by Frank Lawrence Owsley. This densely researched work explores the dominance of cotton in the economic and political life of the South during the Civil War and the period preceding it. The reader is particularly referred to the section dealing with the blockade of Southern ports by the Union Navy.

The Impending Crisis of the South: How to Meet It by Hinton Rowan Helper. Helper's forebears lived in the South for a hundred years. He, too, was born there and lived in North Carolina. His book, published in 1857, created a sensation. In it he advanced the thesis that the small minority of slaveholders wielded the official power of the South and legislated against five million Southern white farmers, mechanics and yeomen. Further, slavery as an institution prevented the South from achieving its potential growth. He proposed that the economic well-

[180]

being and social health of the South demanded the immediate abolition of slavery.

5. THE MOUNTAIN PEOPLE OF THE SOUTH DUR-
ING THE CIVIL WAR:
Desertion During the Civil War by Ella Lonn, *Disloyalty
in the Confederacy* by Georgia Lee Tatum, and *Conscription and Conflict in the Confederacy* by Albert Burton
Moore. These three books listed in the order of preference,
tell how the mountain people of Virginia, North and South
Carolina, Georgia, Alabama and Tennessee organized
counter-measures against the Confederacy. Provocative
material.

6. GENERAL:
The Mason Report. On December 14, 1859, twelve days
after John Brown was hanged, the Congress of the United
States appointed a committee to "Inquire Into The Facts
Attending The Late Invasion And Seizure Of The United
States Army At Harper's Ferry, Virginia." Senator James
M. Mason of Virginia was Chairman of the Congressional
Committee; Senator Jefferson Davis of Mississippi, future
President of the Confederacy, was also a member. The
Mason Report contains many interesting eye-witness ac-
counts of the raid, plus numerous valuable documents
conveniently brought together in one volume.
A *John Brown Reader* edited and with commentary by
Louis Ruchames. An excellent collection of documents
by and about John Brown with equally excellent introduc-
tions to the documents by the editor. In the back of the
book there is a section "Guides to Documents Used,"
wherein is listed much source material.

INDEX

[187]

White, The Reverend Martin, 54, 57

Whitman, Walt, 75, 167, 171

Whittier, John Greenleaf, 167

Wilberforce Institute, 72

Wilberforce Settlement, 72

Wilkinson, Allen, 50, 51

Williams, H. H., 49, 52

Wise, Governor Henry A., 119, 123, 127, 134, 142, 147–148, 157–158, 165, 170, 173; *see also illustration insert 148*

Women's Rights Convention, 64

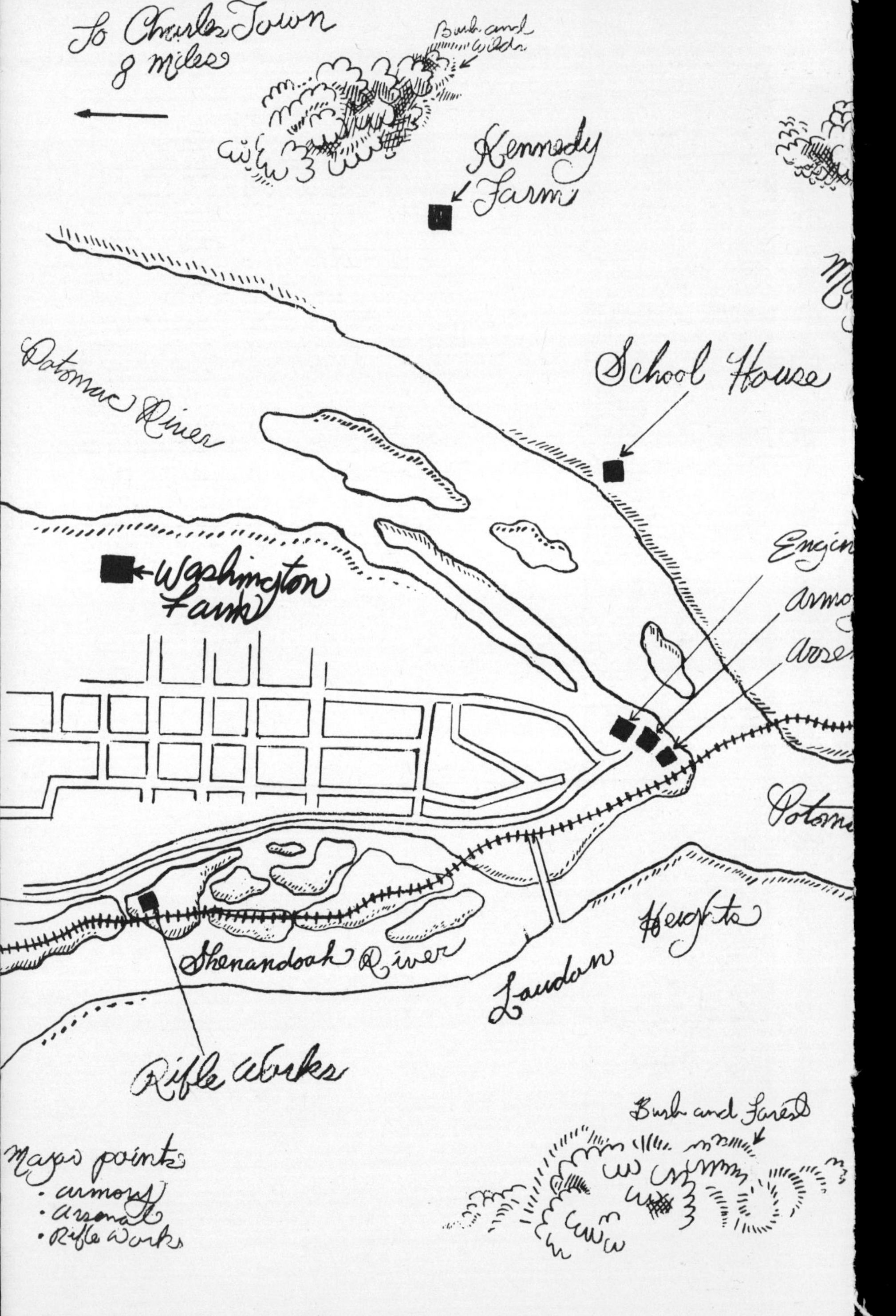

To Charles Town
8 miles

Barb. and Wildn.

Kennedy Farm

School House

Potomac River

Engine
Armory
Arsenal

Washington Farm

Potomac

Shenandoah River

Loudon Heights

Rifle Works

Burb and Forest

Major points
• armory
• arsenal
• Rifle Works